THE PHOTO TRANSFER HANDBOOK

Jean Ray Laury

SNAP IT,

PRINT IT,

STITCH IT!

 C&T PUBLISHING

©1999 Jean Ray Laury
Illustrations©1999 C&T Publishing, Inc.

Editor: Liz Aneloski
Technical Editor: Vera Tobin
Copy Editor: Vera Tobin
Book Designer: Ewa Gavrielov
Cover Designer: Christina Jarumay
Design Director: Kathy Lee
Illustrators: John Cram & Jay Richards
Photographer: E. Z. Smith, unless otherwise noted
Published by C&T Publishing, Inc., P.O. Box 1456, Lafayette, California 94549

Attention Teachers:
C&T Publishing, Inc. encourages you to use this book as a text for teaching. Contact us at 800-284-1114 or www.ctpub.com for more information about the C&T Teachers Program.

We take great care to ensure that the information included in this book is accurate and presented in good faith, but no warranty is provided nor results guaranteed. Since we have no control over the choice of materials or procedures used, neither the author nor C&T Publishing, Inc. shall have any liability to any person or entity with respect to any loss or damage caused directly or indirectly by the information contained in this book.

Trademarked (™) and Registered Trademarked (®) names are used throughout this book. Rather than use the symbols with every occurance of a trademark and registered trademark name, we are using the names only in an editorial fashion and to the benefit of the owner, with no intention of infringement.

Library of Congress Cataloging-in-Publication Data

Laury, Jean Ray.
    The photo transfer handbook : snap it, print it, stitch it / Jean Ray Laury.
            p.   cm.
    Includes bibliographical references and index.
    ISBN 1-57120-064-9 (pbk.)
    1. Transfer-printing   2. Textile printing   3. Iron-on transfers. 4. Quilting.   I. Title.
TT852.7.L38 1999
746'.04--dc21   98-38813
                                                CIP

Printed in Hong Kong
10   9   8   7   6   5   4   3   2   1

contents

acknowledgments

Several wonderful assistants, whose high spirits never flagged, saw me through the writing of this book. I especially thank Jackie Vermeer (who not only worked long hours herself, but by example made me stick to my writing). I thank Lizabeth Laury for her resourcefulness and energy, and for rescuing my syntax. And thanks to Susan Smeltzer, whose computer savvy far exceeds mine (not a great challenge). She is always ready to explore some new process.

Most of all I thank the quilters and designers whose work is the heart and spirit of this book.

Thanks to Liz Aneloski, a great editor, to Kathy Lee, and to Ewa Gavrielov who designed this colorful book.

And thanks to Frank, whose culinary skills and sense of the ridiculous supplied great food and humor.

introduction

With photo processes, every quilter becomes an alchemist, transferring images of her garden, her grandmother, her four-year-old child, or her entire family album onto a quilt. Anything that can be copied can be transferred—photographs, flowers, your roommate's traffic tickets (certainly not yours), letters, the final payment on your house, or a favorite piece of needlework. The transfers, in full color, single color, or black-and-white, yield remarkably detailed photo likenesses. The process is fun and it's easy.

The purpose of this book is four-fold:

1. To introduce you to the magical world of photo transfer and to give you step-by-step instructions for the process.
2. To inspire you by sharing the work of many quilters, artists, and surface designers (some beginners and others experienced) working in this medium.
3. To give step-by-step instructions for projects to help you create your first photo transfer masterpiece.
4. To offer information on products and sources as well as for mail-order photo-to-fabric companies.

Several quilts in this book are first forays into the transfer process; others leave us transfixed and wide-eyed over the inventive and artistic uses of this commonly available technical process. Included are examples of what you can do even if you do not own a computer or have no access to a copy shop. There is also inspiration for those who are already expert at running their computers.

I am not a computer expert. I'm a quilter, designer, and teacher. While I'm willing to share everything I know, I certainly don't know everything about anything. However, I'm excited and enthusiastic about the photo transfer process. It has tremendous potential for creative use. The learning never ends.

If you are not computer literate, you can still work with many of these processes. There are color photocopy machines in even the smallest of towns, and mail-order sources are available to everyone. Either one of these can transfer images to fabric for you.

If you are already computer literate, many of these processes will be simple for you. If not, taking classes is a tremendous help. Personally, I am somewhat impatient with classes. There is so much infor-

mation in which I have little personal interest and which I do not intend to use. I find it more helpful to hire someone who has the expertise to show me how to accomplish the specific things I want to do. In the long run that may be less expensive and is certainly less time consuming.

It does take time and attention to learn the skills necessary to manipulate photos or images (as you learn, make notes on page 80 of this book). However, wonderful things can be accomplished by a beginner with an absolute minimum of experience!

While initially some quilters are a bit intimidated by the high-tech feel of computer generated images or photo transfers, my guess is that anyone who runs a sewing machine can learn photo transfer techniques with ease.

about copyright

When you see an image you like, it's pretty inviting to just slap it down on a copier, press the copy button and use it in your next quilt. It's possible to copy just about anything, but you may be violating copyright, making it illegal and unethical to do so.

You can identify copyrighted works by the appearance of the © symbol, followed by a name and the year. In the case of magazines and books, the whole publication will be copyrighted.

Photographers hold the copyright on every photograph they take unless specified otherwise in writing.

There are several points to remember:

1. Many copyright-free sources are available to you from which you can print any image you like. Dover Publications clearly identifies which of their books are free of copyright restrictions. Books full of "clip art" are available. Thousands of different computer "click art" images are available. Some allow one-time use, some allow unlimited use and others may be limited to items not for sale. Read each for specific limits.

2. The copyrights of materials published over fifty years ago will have expired. However, copyrights are renewable, and if the company is still in business or the image is still in use, the protection will almost certainly be current.

3. You can often get permission to use copyrighted images, but you must get it in writing. Call the Public Relations or Legal Services Department of the company and explain how you intend to use the image. If they do not respond try writing to them, sending a brief letter stating what you want. Enclose a self-addressed stamped postcard, already filled out, so all the recipient has to do is check a box and sign his or her name. You need the name because you may be asked to acknowledge the source of permission when you use the material.

4. Point-and-shoot or instant cameras, as well as throw-away cameras, can take most of the uncertainty and much of the expense out of taking your own photos. Keep a small camera in your car so you are always ready to record something that intrigues, inspires, or amuses you.

5. There are photographs available through photo services (see page 76), as well as through other sources, such as the Library of Congress or NASA. The reference desk at your local library can help you locate national services. Check your yellow page directory for a local photo service or archive. Some of these addresses appear at the back of this book on page 76.

6. Finally, remember that copyrights were created to protect the artist, designer, or creator of an image. That means the law is there to protect you too, not to restrict you. If you have developed an image which you would like to keep (whether or not you plan to make commercial use of it), you can copyright it. Place the copyright symbol, plus your name and the year, on the work itself. Then, to register it, write for form VA at the Register of Copyrights (see page 76). There is a small registration fee and a relatively simple form to fill out to copyright your work. The designs can be "ganged." For example, if you are printing cards of three of your quilts and wish to record the copyright, all three can be placed on one sheet and registered for one fee.

Even if you don't register your copyright, you are covered for a period of several months. The symbol may serve to remind another viewer that this material belongs to you. If you have an image which has commercial potential, it will be advantageous to copyright it.

CHAPTER 1
about photo transfers

Basic Information

Photo transfer of images is a simple, direct way to work, allowing photographic results on fabric without the use of a darkroom. It doesn't involve mixing powders or chemicals and produces results that can't be duplicated any other way.

> "Photo transfer is by far the fastest and simplest method to use and there is little that can go wrong."
>
> – Alvena Hall, Australian quilter

Photo transfer is available to everyone. If you do not have a computer/printer at home, all you need is access to a copy shop, and you can manage without a copy shop if you use mail order. You do need an iron if you choose to do your own transfers. If you have a computer and printer you are already set up to print cloth on your inkjet printer. It's an intriguing process, either way.

> "The work by Photo Textiles (Aneta Sperber, magic woman) is very dependable and I prefer to use them for commissions. This past year I have begun doing some iron-on images via my Canon inkjet printer and their transfer paper which gives me much more freedom."
>
> – Sandra Sider, quilt artist

Photo transfer is not always easy and there are expenses involved, but you can create effects in home studios with transfers that are not available by any other means.

It is easy to adjust, retouch, or trim a photo to eliminate unwanted parts. This visual editing (which is the most fun part of the process) can be accomplished on the prints or copies as well as on the transfer sheets, leaving your original intact. You can snip out an image of yourself so you fly with the Wright brothers or snuggle up to Matisse. You could give

These pillows by the author are inkjet transfers using small snapshots that were enlarged for use. The first, enlarged from a group photo, was trimmed to leave a white border. On the next, a black-and-white photo was printed in sepia and transferred to white fabric. Last, a photo was trimmed to exclude a distracting background.

your uncle a red neck or place yourself alongside John Muir and Teddy Roosevelt atop Half Dome, but don't forget to get permission for copyrighted images (see page 6).

> "A professor who really influenced me told me I couldn't draw and that I should consider myself a Grandma Moses of sorts. So I don't draw—I alter, exchange, reduce, enlarge, add, and subtract from appropriated images. I'm still a little girl, cutting out paper dolls (for images of women) and sneaking *Playboy* magazines out of the dumpster (for images of men). A fashionably posed male paper doll was impossible to find (but no problem in *Playboy* ads)."
>
> – Wendy Huhn

Methods

Two basic transfer methods are commonly available to almost every quilter. One can be accomplished at a copy shop or by mail order; the other can be accomplished at home with a computer and an inkjet printer. All the pieces in this book used transfers made by one method or the other. Methods discussed in this book include:

I. PHOTOCOPY MACHINES: The color laser copier (or CLC), available at copy shops. See Chapter 2, Using a Color Laser Copier, beginning on page 20.
II. COMPUTER PRINTERS: The inkjet or bubble jet printer (the most common home color printer). See Chapter 3, Using a Computer Printer, beginning on page 27.

It is important to make a distinction between the photocopy machine and the computer printer. A photocopy machine uses toner set with heat, and an inkjet or bubble jet uses ink and no heat. When you go to a copy shop to have a photo transfer made they will use a color laser copier. If you print on transfer paper at home, you undoubtedly will be using a color computer printer. Each uses its own papers and it is important to keep these identified and separate.

Almost all transfer papers can be used at home with a hot iron or a heat press to transfer the image to fabric.

Many transfer papers have identifying marks on the back. The green striped one on the left is for inkjet printers. The Magic Touch paper on the right is for CLC. Be sure to identify any papers that come unmarked.

Important Information

The following information is for any transfers—whether you use the CLC or inkjet.

Original

Your original can be anything you can photocopy or scan—leaves, buttons, diplomas, fabric, etc. The single most popular original, a favorite with almost everyone, is the photograph.

If you take your own photographs you have control over the images and you don't have to worry about copyright issues. Besides traditional film developing, you can send your exposed but undeveloped film to a company that will transfer your film to computer disc or CD-ROM, so you can print your photos from your computer. If you prefer, they'll download your images directly to your computer through e-mail. New digital cameras can provide information to be fed directly into your computer, from which you can print images.

"I work on my computer every morning and sometimes all day. I plan to do this all of my life, and if I go into a nursing home it had better be electronically wired.

Having a computer is as good as eating ice cream all day long and not gaining weight. Processes that used to require hours of painstaking work in the dark room now can be accomplished with the computer in only minutes."

– Gail Chase, photographer and quilt artist

The clearer your original, the better your transfer will be. Select photos with good contrast between the featured attraction and the background. A fuzzy or blurry photo will produce a fuzzy, blurry print. Whenever you are uncertain of your photo quality, make a copy or a print on plain paper before doing the transfer.

If the color of your original is not accurately reproduced, you must make an adjustment either on the color laser copier or on your computer software.

If the background adds nothing to your image you can remove it from your copy or print (scissors work fine) and place the cut-out on fabric. Large areas of nondescript or colorless background area will not enhance your photo.

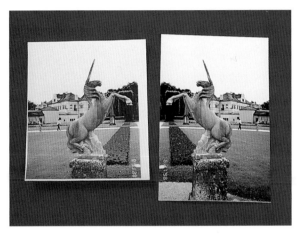

The large photo on the right was scanned to produce the transfer at left, it was then trimmed to a smaller size before the background was cut away. Colors may brighten in the transfer process.

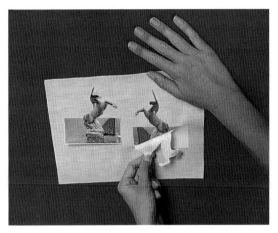

The image on transfer paper (on the left) was trimmed to eliminate distracting background. On the right, the transfer paper is being peeled away after heat setting to fabric.

An unmodified photo transfer of the sisters on a peach colored cloth.

Unwanted background can be cut away before transfering to fabric.

Choosing and Using the Images

You can use photos of all kinds and sizes (by enlarging, reducing, or trimming). To create your own memory quilt, first check out your family albums and boxes of photos. Even if some are black-and-white and some are color, they'll still work together. Combined with brightly colored fabrics, the differences seem insignificant. With pastel colors, the differences will be more obvious.

Color can be added to black-and-white photographs in any of several ways. Check the chapters on CLC (beginning on page 20) or inkjet (beginning on page 27), depending on which method you are using.

There are dozens of ways to approach the design of a quilt. Here are a few suggestions so you are not overwhelmed by stacks of old family pictures:

1. Collect the photos and memorabilia of just one person.
2. Select family members with a particular relationship to you—all of your grandparents, aunts and uncles, or children.
3. Choose all family wedding pictures.
4. Chronologically arrange photos, records, and papers belonging to one person.
5. Use images of your hometown.
6. Select photos of the houses in which you have lived.
7. Assemble pictures of your pets, vacations, celebrations, flower gardens, kids in uniforms, swim meets, or holidays.
8. Use drawings or paintings made by children.
9. Make a quilt about your grandmother's cookie jar—take a picture of the jar itself, her rolling pin, her recipe, her wearing an apron, and, of course, the cookies. This may provide a quilt as nostalgic as one full of portraits.

You'll come up with many more ideas as you sift through boxes of photos or family papers.

Jan Hirth made over 250 transfers when she organized a quilt-in for a family reunion. The photos were brought already copied onto various transfer papers, using a range of copiers. While they had some failures, they did end up with fifteen transfers on each of fifteen quilts—225 in all, or nine out of ten. She eventually used a thirty-five second heat setting, moved the iron to avoid steam-vent marks, and always allowed one to two minutes for the iron to re-heat between transfers.

Once you have collected the images you intend to use, you'll need to determine how to arrange them. This book is full of wonderful inspiration and ideas. Traditional quilt blocks will work if you are willing to adjust the sizes of your photos to fit the blocks. Or you can select a block made from pieces of varying sizes and use photos in all of the pieces. It's also possible to just outline each transfer with color and pattern to create blocks of a consistent size, as in a Log Cabin block. Once you have an idea of how you'll use the transfers you'll know whether or not you need to alter the sizes.

Reversal

When transfers are heat set to fabric, they will be reversed unless the mirror-image or reversal option is used when copying or printing the original. When you compare the original to the image on transfer paper, the paper should be a left-right reversal of the original. When transferred, it reverses again and will appear "right," matching the original. Most copy shops will do this reversal without your asking. If your original is a slide, be sure to indicate right and left. On some images, such as clouds, trees, or the ocean, reversal won't matter. On others, it will. A reversal would shift the Statue of Liberty's torch from one hand to the other. Your friend, a right-handed bowler, will appear to be holding the ball in her left hand on the transfer paper. Most CLCs and computers have reversal capabilities.

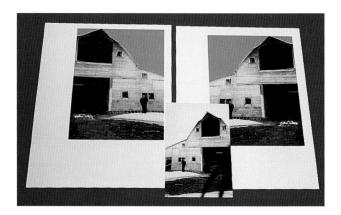

The original photo is shown in the center. On the left is the image on transfer paper (it appears reversed). The finished transfer (at right) reads like the original.

A paper collage original was scanned and printed on transfer paper after it was reduced. One image was reversed and one was not.

Jan Krentz pieced together two first-day-of-school photos so she could have one shot showing all three children. By cutting around one edge of the girl she was able to slide the photos together to make a composite.

The fish heat set to fabric.

Collage

By grouping individual photos or rearranging parts of family photos, you can collect people from different centuries or various countries. You could unite a half dozen generations of your family into one picture.

To make economical use of the photo transfer paper, place as many images on the glass plate, the scanner plate, or the computer screen as will fit within the format of the page size. If you are going to make a collage for the photocopy, first duplicate your photos onto a sheet of plain copy paper. This copy can then be cut up and reassembled or collaged. (This process can be done electronically on the computer, but it may be time-consuming.) The collage is then used to put the image on transfer paper. By always working with prints or copies your original remains untouched.

Photos can be cut up and reassembled.

Group your photos, drawings, and words to make efficient use of a single sheet of transfer paper. Note that all prints are reversals of the originals.

Costs

Costs of transfer paper and commercial heat setting vary greatly, so if you are making numerous images you'll want to check prices from different sources. Costs vary depending on quantity purchased, brand, and source.

Jackie Vermeer commented that the CLC transfers for David's Family (page 42) cost her slightly over $50. She carefully grouped photos to make efficient use of the transfer paper. "Cost is part of working with photos. Just make the most of each transfer and don't waste money on poor photos."

"It is just the cost of my art supplies. Unless you have what you need available you are limiting your palette and creativity. If you had to justify all your expenditures you would never get started. I've printed enough color transfers, probably seventy-five, for several quilts and am still on my first ink cartridge."

– Susan Smeltzer, quilt artist

Artists who do lots of transfers and have made careful comparisons conclude that the difference in cost of inkjet printer transfers and CLC transfers is minimal. The primary advantage of inkjet is working at home, at any time of the day or night.

Transfer papers purchased in quantity (a box of 50, 100, or a ream) will cost less. Initially, however, packets of two sheets will let you try a variety of brands. Don't buy a quantity until you know that the copy shops most convenient to you will use your paper. Buy a quantity for the inkjet printer only after you have tested several different transfer papers.

Most office suppliers carry several brands of transfer paper (for both CLC and inkjet). Not all suppliers stock them and not all of them will have a variety. Prices and brands keep changing, so always check. Prices as well as the types of transfer papers used in chain copy shops vary significantly from one shop to the next.

Color

A black-and-white photo can be printed with additional color on either the color laser copier or computer printer. You might, for example, use a sepia tone, or duplicate the black-and-white original in only blue and black or only red and black.

> "I get so excited every time I make a transfer. I can hardly wait to pull the paper off. The vivid colors are the best part."
>
> – Jackie Vermeer, quilt artist

Another option is to transfer to colored fabric. Remember that the light areas in your photo (for example a white shirt) will let the fabric color come through. Printed only in black on white fabric, the shirt will appear white. Printed only in black on a yellow fabric, the shirt will appear yellow. If you choose to print on colors other than white, be certain to select a light color of fabric.

One photo was printed on transfer paper in its original color. The others show combinations of a single color (blue, red, or yellow with black). The print with a brownish cast was a mixture of red and green inks.

Surface

The surface appearance of the fabric after the image has been transferred may vary slightly from one brand of transfer paper to another and from one process to another. Some brands give a dull finish and are relatively soft. Others have more sheen and seem stiffer. Everyone seems to have a theory about this. One designer insists she gets the best results when using Dharma's transfer paper on a Xerox color copier. The next person swears by a Canon printer using Canon paper. Perhaps the age of the machine makes a difference, and obviously the brand of paper and copier also have an effect. It is important to copy a single photograph using the assorted papers and machines available to you and determine your preference. No single answer works for everyone. There are too many variables. Some quilters are primarily concerned about the feel or "hand" of the fabric, while for others color is the crucial element. Make notes on page 80 to keep track of your findings.

> "I used a **CLC** and a home iron on my first project and found the process quite simple—and the fabric very soft and flexible."
>
> – Lilly Thorne, quilt artist

New Products

New papers keep coming on the market, though many will be made by a single manufacturer and sold under different names.

By the time this book is published, Air-Waves will have a new paper available. Xerox's paper is a relative newcomer on the market. G&S will have a paper designed especially for hand-ironing. Cool-peel or E-Z peel papers can be peeled after the heat has dissipated (easier on your fingers). Watch for new products, as they seem to be arriving in a pretty steady stream. And we all await new inkjet inks that will be permanent on fabric.

Fabric

White or light-colored fabrics provide the best base for transfers since the fabric color will show through any open or white areas of your photo. The light area in a photo is not printed white, but is rather an unpigmented area (like the clear areas on a negative). Using a white fabric will most nearly replicate the original photo. If you have a photo in which a white cat with black eyes and collar is shown, and it is transferred to red fabric, the cat will appear as red with black eyes and collar. Fabric color will show through in all light areas. The transfer to most dark-colored fabrics will almost obliterate the image. Pastels and other light values will work almost as well as white for a readable image. I love using tiny polka dots or soft stripes.

Using a finely-woven (200 thread count) fabric will result in sharper transfers. Avoid rough weaves (like natural linens) or nubby fabrics, unless your special need for texture overrides your interest in clarity or readability. While most manufacturers recommend all cotton, many quilters use a cotton/poly blend. Test your fabric to make sure it will withstand heat setting. If a particular fabric is not taking transfers well, wash it first in Synthropol or a vinegar rinse. Some fabric finishes may resist the transfer, though most fabrics do not have this problem.

One quilter used sateen and preferred it to all other fabrics. She maintained that she "could not make a bad print."

G&S carries a product called PAROopaque, developed for printing on black or dark colors. It provides a light backing for the transfer and this goes over the dark fabric. Its disadvantage is that it gives a somewhat plastic, almost rubbery surface. While not preferable for quilts or garments, it has some application for wall pieces. Air Waves' One Step Opaque works similarly for transfers to dark fabric.

> "I really enjoy printing my own fabric on the computer. It is rather labor intensive, but the results are always worthwhile.... I love creating images on the computer; it's like a 'power tool for the mind.'"
>
> – Becky Sundquist, quilt artist

Quilting

Transfers leave a somewhat plasticized surface, and it is not easy to hand quilt through this extra thickness. Jackie Vermeer quilted her piece (page 42) by hand, but quilted "in the ditch" over seams that were pressed open. She broke two needles before finishing. For hand quilting, either press all seam allowances away from where the quilting will be, or press seams open when joining two transfers.

> "I find it relatively easy to stitch over transfers. Use quality thread and just slow down a bit."
>
> – Susan Smeltzer, machine quilting teacher

Several machine quilters used quilted lines like drawings over their transfers and found that the extra body provided by transfer actually made the fabric easier to handle.

If you really object to the change in the hand of the fabric, consider using dye transfer, photo silkscreen, or blue printing, all of which are thoroughly covered in my book *Imagery on Fabric*.

Detail of FAN COAT by Louise Thompson (garment on page 54). This segmented look was created by ironing a transfer over fabrics pieced to a foundation. The original was an old postcard from the Orient.

Detail of GRANDMA'S 100TH BIRTHDAY QUILT by Martie Carroll (full quilt page 29). Using her sewing machine as a drawing tool, Martie has outlined the figures in the photo transfers, then filled in the background area with patterns of quilting stitches. Outer pieced areas are lightly quilted.

Detail of TROPHIES by Sue Pierce (full quilt page 43). The photo transfer was machine quilted with stitches that outlined the hands and the toddler. The quilting not only highlights the figure, but adds detail which helps break up the large photo transfer area.

This quilt label includes a transfer of the young quiltmaker as well as her name and the date. The transfer was trimmed before it was heat set to fabric. The white fabric edge could easily be turned under to the edge of the image for appliqué. If the transfer is left untrimmed the excess transfer material makes the fabric heavier and more difficult to turn under and stitch through.

Detail of tubular container for *Oliver's Battery* by Sharon Doyle (full quilt page 59).

Kathleen Deneris's quilt (page 48) includes a label portraying the young artists. The photo transfer was trimmed, then appliquéd to the quilt back.

The quilt label from *Peace'd Together* by Susan E. Brown (page 21) includes information along with a pattern created from snippets of photo transfer paper.

Quilt Labels

Quilt labels are being changed entirely through the use of transfers. Now they can be so personal that your photo can become part of the documented information.

Sharon Doyle made a tubular container (page 16) for her quilt before mailing it to a show and then to a buyer. The photo on the container is a replica of the one used in her quilt. Information was added with permanent marker.

Kathleen Deneris has used not only her grandchildren's drawings, but photos of the children also.

Variations

Here are some simple ways to create variations in the transfers, many of which you'll see in work throughout this book.

A. Transfer the images to light-colored fabrics (beiges, pinks, pastels).

B. Transfer to polka dots, light florals, stripes, or hand-dyed fabrics.

C. Cut away extraneous areas of the photos, so an image is silhouetted against a colored background or blue sky.

D. Separate or segment a face by cutting the transfer into checkerboard, horizontal stripes, or vertical bands before it is transferred to fabric.

E. Set the print into a traditional block. Log Cabin (see page 70), Baby Blocks, Sawtooth Stars (see page 73) and Attic Windows all work well.

F. Transferring to wood opens a Pandora's box of possibilities. Nothing is safe if a transfer artist gets her hands on it! Wood accepts photo transfer, but it is rather touchy. The wood must be very smooth, and little hobby shop boxes in a clear, almost-white wood worked best for me. I found the inkjet transfers the most difficult, since the transfer, when heated, tends to slide around on the wood. It is difficult not to smear the image. CLC transfers do not get slippery on wood and are therefore easier to handle. Practice on scraps of wood first. Any grain or other irregularities will interfere with the transfer.

G. Individualize dolls by using the face of a loved one.

H. Use a favorite image and transfer it to a computer mouse pad.

I. Transfer one image over another to create a multi-layered look.

J. Soften edges or areas of a transfer print (before heat transfer) with the use of a solvent (acetone).

Fish is an inkjet transfer on 4" x 6" box.
Photo of two figures is a CLC transfer on 4" square box.

HANNAH BABY
by Jackie Vermeer, 33" high.
    The astonishingly realistic appearance of this doll resulted from the use of a photo transferred onto One Step paper with a CLC. It was heat set on muslin using a home iron. A ready-made stuffed doll from a hobby store provided the base to which the face was stitched and a hair-piece from the dollar store added the final touch.

The faces of these dolls by the author were transferred to white fabric, which was then cut out and hand appliquéd to the doll head. Be sure to measure, then enlarge or reduce the photo when making the transfer. When the proportions are a bit off the faces are funnier. A face transfer with slightly large features makes it easier to see the face details.

SISTERS
by Jackie Vermeer, 11" x 8½".
   A standard computer mouse pad was personalized with
a photo transfer. The polyurethane pad has a fabric cover to
which the image was transferred. This was the only non-
brightly colored pad which Jackie found, and the resulting
image is muted and soft.

transfers using a color laser copier

The marvelous magic of photo transfers by color laser copier (CLC) is as near as your closest copy shop. All you need is your original, a special transfer paper onto which your original will be copied, access to a CLC, and the heat and pressure required to transfer the image to cloth.

The success of your CLC transfer to fabric will be affected by several variables.

Photo Transfer Papers

Photo transfer papers (or heat transfer sheets) are polymer-coated papers which can be fed into a color laser copier and permanently heat set to cloth. The transfers are vivid and the process is not difficult.

Some copy shops will print on transfer papers you bring in to them; others will work only with their own papers. This reluctance to use other transfer papers is because warranties may not apply to their CLCs if transfer papers other than in-house stock are used. Be sure to check this out with your favorite copy shop before you invest in a ream of transfer papers.

It is less expensive to supply your own transfer sheets, but they must be compatible with the CLC you use and acceptable to the copy shop. Different papers have been formulated for different machines; however, many are interchangeable and seem to work on any copier, with either hand ironing or heat press. Bonnie Peterson likes using a combination of heat press and hand ironing, often in a single piece, to create an effect of greater depth. She finds the heat-pressed images to be crisper, while the hand ironed are more translucent. Perform your own experiments and make notes on page 80.

Paper made for your inkjet printer will NOT work in a color laser copier, and will in fact cause real havoc. Do not mix the two. It is a good idea to identify the paper and its use on the box or package in which it is stored.

HEAT TRANSFER SHEETS FOR COLOR COPY TRANSFER
(8.5" X 11", 11" x 14", and 11" x 17")

	Sources (by list number, see page 76)
Air Waves' ONE STEP	(1, 4, 6)
Canon	(1, 4 , 5, 7)
Inktron	(1)
Magic Transfer	(4, 10)
Mirror Image	(1)
PAROopaque	(4, 12)
PARO P (Press)	(4, 8, 12)
PARO P (Iron)	(4, 8, 12)
Paroply	(1)
Photo Effects	(2, 3)
The Magic Touch	(1)
Xerox Transfer Paper	(5, 16)
	(suppliers vary)

Choosing Images

Some quilters want to take their photos into the copy shop and walk out with the finished fabric. Others like a "hands on" active involvement with the transfer process. Certainly the latter allows you more leeway and time to get creative with the photos. For example, if you want to pair the left half of your own portrait with the right half of your mother's taken when she was the same age, you'll need to do that at home. If you're going to put your best friend's face on Venus de Milo's body, the copy shop isn't going to cut and collage it for you. Many do, however, provide a workspace, scissors, paper cutter, etc. for your use.

Your originals can be 35mm slides, photos, documents, snapshots, clippings, leaves, collages, drawings, or anything else that will lie flat in the copier. Your transfers to cloth will be no better than the originals, so always work with the best quality photos you have. While copy shops can make copies from your 35mm slides, most have no means to project anything larger. Therefore, you may not be able to use 2¼" x 2¼" or 4" x 5" transparencies.

PEACE'D TOGETHER
by Susan E. Brown, 45" x 57".

In a workshop with Deborah Melton Anderson, Susan made a series of variations of a single portrait of herself with her mother and two sisters. Set in a Sister's Choice block, the images change from chaotic on the left to increasing order on the right. After manipulating the images on a CLC, she transferred them from One Step transfer paper on a commercial heat press. The quilt is heavily covered with quilting.

After selecting the special effects button, Susan used a contour option for another variation of the family photo. The photo was cut up and individual portraits were repeated in the quilt.

The photo was altered using a mosaic special effects button on the CLC. This offered variety to the repeated use of a single photo.

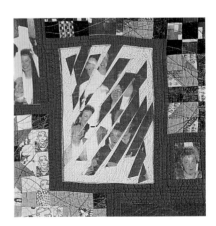

After printing on photo transfer paper, the paper was sliced and reassembled for a further variation. Diagonal quilting lines exaggerate the slashing pattern.

You can also make a collage, by first copying your photos onto sheets of plain copy paper. These copies can then be cut up, reassembled, and copied onto your transfer paper. If you stack or collage the transfers themselves, you create several layers and these varying thicknesses of paper can interfere with the heat transfer to cloth. Lines from the edges of a collage will sometimes appear when the cut edge of one paper overlaps another. To avoid this, make a new copy or print of the collage, or glue all cut edges for the closest possible contact. If lines persist, you may need to eliminate excess hidden layers and abut edges of photos together. Just one single overlap will not usually create a shadow line.

To make economical use of the color photocopier, place as many photographs (or other images) face down on the platen glass as will fit within the chosen paper size. If there is space left on the platen after you lay out your originals, add pieces of solid-color or patterned paper. You can later use these as background fill-ins, or for cutting letters or shapes.

Remember to use the mirror image button when photocopying your images so the images will face the right direction when they are transferred.

Adding Color

If you are starting with black-and-white copies, add color by using permanent markers, colored pencils, or dye sticks. Textile paints or airbrush inks can be used to create soft watercolor effects or a bright graphic look. These colored black-and-white copies can then be copied in color to transfer paper on a CLC.

To add color to the transfer sheet itself (whether black-and-white or color), Pentel Pastel Dye Sticks work well. Berol Prismacolor pencils can be used if you avoid drawing with the point, which may scrape the emulsion. Thinned Versatex paint works for light colors, although small areas are easier to color than larger ones. Felt tip markers make very strong lines and so are not appropriate for all prints. It is easy to tint a black-and-white photo transfer after it has been heat set to cloth. Use thinned paint, but don't heat set with an iron. Let it air cure.

Removing Color

After copying her images onto transfer paper on a color laser copier, Jeanne Weinberg found she could reduce or alter the color by wiping a cloth moistened with acetone over the transfer. This achieved soft, painterly effects and a blurring of the images. In addition, she altered colors by layering one transfer over another. Since the transfers are translucent, not opaque, the result was an overlay of images as well as of colors.

DEER ISLE: A PAINTER'S LANDSCAPE
by Jeanne Norris Weinberg, 12" X 18".
Photo: by Jean Norris Weinberg
   Using a remarkable combination of methods, Jeanne
produced this distinctive panel.

The original photograph at left (top) of grasses at Deer Island,
Maine was copied in a color negative function (or color reversal) onto transfer paper in the color laser copier.

   Jeanne then copied her photo of paintbrushes, taken at
Haystack School of Crafts, in mirror image onto transfer paper.
By stacking the two transfers on a light table, she could read
through them to determine the changes she wanted to make.

   Using an acetone-moistened cloth, she reduced the color
and achieved the soft painterly look she wanted. She then
transferred the image to cloth (heat press at 375 degrees for
eleven seconds). Because the images are translucent, when
she transferred the second photo over the first (same temperature and time) a composite of the two was created (above).

Heat Setting

The Transfer Process at The Copy Shop

Copy shops heat set the transfer paper to fabric using a heat press (or T-shirt press) which gives even pressure and high, even heat. Therefore, the copies transferred on a heat press may be more perfectly transferred than those you do with an iron. They are also more permanent through repeated washings, which may be important if you are making quilts for children—less crucial if you are making a wall piece. It will also be more expensive per transfer, though there will be fewer errors.

There are a few copy shops which do not have their own T-shirt presses (or heat presses) though they will copy your original onto a transfer sheet. You will need to take the copied transfer to a T-shirt shop for heat setting (or do it at home). Still other shops send them out and you come back later to retrieve your transfer to fabric.

Unless you want a T-shirt, or some other article available where the transfer is made, you will need to take your fabric to the copy shop with you. The more smoothly woven the fabric, (a 200 thread count natural fiber is excellent), the more detailed your transfer will be and the fabric must be able to withstand the heat setting temperature of 350 to 375 degrees.

─── **WHAT YOU NEED** ───

- *Original*
- *Pressed fabric*
- *Scissors*

─── **STEPS** ───

1 *Take your pressed fabric and original (photo, collage, etc.) to the copy shop.*

2 *Have the original copied (mirror image) to transfer paper.*

3 *Using scissors, cut away any excess transfer paper surrounding the image (white borders, unwanted background).*

4 *Have the transfer heat set onto your fabric.*

5 *Go to your studio and work (play) with this new fabric.*

☞ **TROUBLESHOOTING FOR TRANSFERS AT THE COPY SHOP**

PROBLEM: *Slight stiffness*

SOLUTION: *There is no real solution. This is the nature of transfer. Compare other brands of paper to see how they affect the hand of the fabric. Washing with Synthropol and soaking in Mil-soft will sometimes soften the transfer. Repeat if necessary.*

PROBLEM: *There is a line, either diagonal or straight, across the transfer.*

SOLUTION: *Be sure the paper is removed with a single steady pull. Do not hesitate or interrupt the pull. Avoid stops. The original may have been imperfect.*

The Transfer Process for Heat Setting at Home (Hot Peel)

Some brands of transfer paper allow for heat-setting at home using either an iron or a heat press. Others require the greater heat and pressure of a commercial press. It's just easier (and more certain) with a commercial or home heat press. Use an Elna press (or any similar press, such as INSTA Shirt press, Euro Pro, Hix, Air Waves, or a Singer press, that can achieve a temperature of 350 to 375 degrees), along with pressure, for 20 to 30 seconds.

While some shops will insist that their transfers must be heat set on a heat press, you may still get excellent transfers with a home iron and some practice.

If possible, find an old iron which will achieve a higher heat level and be free of steam vents. New irons (non-steam) are available, but it will be less costly if you can locate one in a thrift shop or at a yard sale. Directions for most transfer papers recommend no-steam heat setting since moisture interferes with transfer. However, several quilters have used steam and saw no difference. Always iron at the highest temperature the fabric will tolerate (optimum temperature for transfer is 350 to 375 degrees). A technique for heat setting by iron will take time to perfect. With practice, you will discover the right combination of transfer paper, temperature, pressure, timing, and paper removal technique.

WHAT YOU NEED

- *Heat press or iron and solid surface*
- *Fabric to receive transfer*
- *Scissors*

STEPS

1. *Cut away excess transfer material (borders, extra white, extraneous background, or unwanted persons or parts).*

2. *Select a firm surface on which to heat set the transfer (an ironing board is not stable enough for the pressure you must exert). A bread board on a counter, lightly padded and covered with cloth, will do fine. Some designers prefer using a Teflon pressing cloth between transfer and board.*

3. *Turn the iron to its highest setting (cotton/linen) and let it pre-heat for a couple of minutes.*

4. *Place your smoothly pressed fabric on the board, heat it by ironing, and place the transfer face down on top. Press over it to adhere the transfer to the fabric. It should now be very flat. Iron directly on the paper or, if you prefer, use tissue paper or a Teflon pressing cloth over the top.*

5. *Set the iron down on one area of the transfer and press down with all the weight and energy you can muster for maximum pressure and even heat. Iron for 20 to 30 seconds in each area before sliding the iron to the next area.*

6. *Press over the entire transfer one last time so that all areas are hot.*

7. *While the transfer is still hot, lift one corner to test. If the transfer looks good, continue to peel in a single steady motion, avoiding stops and starts. Peel from the top or the bottom, but not from one corner, which can stretch and distort the image.*

Do not let the transfer cool before peeling it. If it does cool, you may have to re-heat it so that it will peel readily. One quilter uses a hair dryer, propped up, to keep her transfer warm as she works. Another pulls the transfer off as she moves the iron away from that area.

Once cooled, the paper is less flexible and almost impossible to peel, so if you get interrupted, you may have to re-iron the surface.

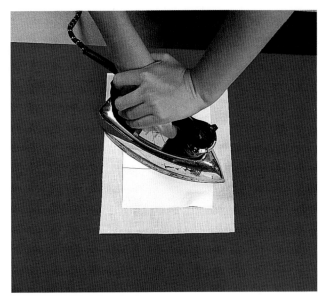

Use pressure as well as high heat to accomplish the transfer. A flat sole-plate iron will work best. With a steam iron the vents may impose a pattern on the transfer if you don't keep the iron moving.

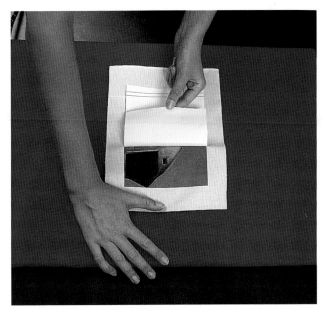

Peel the transfer paper away with the grain of the fabric (not on the diagonal) and peel it in one long, steady pull.

The Transfer Process for Heat Setting at Home (Cool Peel)

Use the same process as for hot peel, steps 1 through 5. Let the transfer sheet cool, then peel.

☞ **TROUBLESHOOTING FOR HEAT SETTING TRANSFER SHEETS AT HOME**

PROBLEM: *Image is incomplete or has not adhered well.*
SOLUTION: *Apply greater pressure.*
Use higher temperature for a longer time.
Use a prewashed and pressed fabric free of finishes.
Use smaller images, at least initially.
Use finer fabric.
Try another brand of paper.

PROBLEM: *There is a line through the transferred image.*
SOLUTION: *Be sure you remove the paper with a single steady pull. Do not hesitate or interrupt the pull. Avoid stops.*
The original may have been imperfect.

PROBLEM: *Inaccurate colors.*
SOLUTION: *Try another copier.*
Adjust colors on the CLC.
Remember that most transfers end up looking a little darker than the original.

CHAPTER 3
transfers using a computer inkjet printer

Changing technology is catapulting quilting into the 21st century, and quilters now position their computers, scanners, and printers right next to their sewing machines. The possibilities for including photos, words, and drawings in our quilts seem unlimited and irresistible. Quilters are determined to convince their printers to do things they were never designed to do—and finding remarkable success.

Equipment
The success of your inkjet transfer to fabric will be affected by several variables.

Inkjet Printers
The Bubble Jet (Canon), DeskJet (HP), Apple, Epson, and all other inkjets come under our general term of inkjet printers. Inkjet printers (with few exceptions) use water-soluble rather than alcohol-based inks. The colors are non-permanent (ever dribble your tea on an inkjet print?). If you have run a piece of muslin through your inkjet printer, undoubtedly you watched the luscious colors wash right down the drain as the fabric was rinsed. Attempts by textile artists to make these transient, ephemeral colors permanent have had varied and limited success. Inkjet printers were made to print on paper and we want to make them work on fabric.

Printers vary not just from one brand to another, but from one series to another within a single brand. For example, some reproduce reds less accurately than others. Newer printers boast the capacity to print more accurate or realistic skin tones, but every printer is different. You will need to use your computer software to adjust them as best you can. What you see on the screen is not necessarily what you will get from your printer; there is a calibration adjustment which can help your printer more accurately interpret the scanned image. Check your owner's manual or call the manufacturer for guidance. Beyond that it may be necessary to enhance certain colors by hand (colored pencils, paint, etc.).

Your printer deposits ink in a pattern of dots per inch (dpi) which determines resolution. The higher the resolution, the sharper the image and the more memory it takes. The smaller the image, the easier it is to work with, so select and scan only the parts of the photograph you want. As you magnify an image, you will reach a point where the pixels (dots or units of ink) enlarge and you get fuzzy edges or small squares. To avoid this, if you still plan to use that particular printer, the image will have to be reduced in size to maintain clarity. By printing on "economy" or "draft" instead of "best" under the print quality option you will deposit less excess ink. "Best" deposits more ink, and because the transfer paper absorbs so little ink, the excess may just collect on the surface and definition will be lost in the transfer.

Scanners
To print and transfer your own drawings, photographs, or flat objects at home you will need a scanner in addition to a computer and an inkjet printer. A scanner is a machine that reads or "scans" an image and then places it on your computer screen. Without the scanner, you can still select from thousands of copyright-free images available on CD and print text directly from your computer.

Scanners vary in terms of the image size they can scan, but a flat-bed allows full-size pages to be scanned. Inexpensive scanners are available, but it will be important to select one with at least 300 optical dpi for good resolution. Scanners come with some software to use them. The software program will have a color saturation option by which the color intensities can be varied. Most programs will also let you make selections for brightness/contrast and color balance. You may want an additional graphics program, although that requires a lot of memory on your computer.

Scanning an image is the fastest way of getting your original into a computer. You do not need very sophisticated equipment to do photo transfer. Scanning photos gobbles up computer memory at an alarming rate, however, and the more you know about your computer, the less likely you are to encounter glitches. Greater familiarity with your program means you can better control your files, expand your design options, and reduce the possibility of crashes. It will require time and diligence to master your software. Photographer Gail Chase suggests that it may be faster and easier to hire a software person to do specific tasks. Some software programs are expensive and complex to learn.

If you don't have a scanner, but your computer has fax capability, you can go to a copy shop and fax your art to your own computer. The fax software can be used to save the transmission as a graphics file from which you can print.

Another option is to take a roll of print or slide film, send your exposed film to Seattle Filmworks (or any company that offers this service) and have it developed on a diskette. Then you can slip the diskette into your computer and work with those images for printing onto transfer papers.

With a scanner, you can use natural objects as well as photos or text. Scan documents, flowers, leaves, seed packets, love letters, embroidery, quilt blocks, and textiles.

Photo Transfer Papers

Special transfer papers made for inkjet printers allow for the transfer of images to fabric with a home iron. Inkjet printers do not use heat when putting the image onto the transfer paper. Photocopy machines (including CLCs) do use heat when putting the image onto the transfer paper. Therefore, the transfer papers for the two should not be confused. Always label any loose transfer sheets, or keep them in the package in which you bought them. If you mistakenly run a CLC transfer paper through your inkjet printer, the ink will just bead up or puddle on the surface, which repels water-based ink, but it will not ruin your printer. An inkjet transfer run through the CLC, however, will have more disastrous results.

A good place to start is to buy the transfer paper made by your printer's manufacturer. The instructions may list specific printers for which they are designed. TR-101, for example, was made specifically for Canon printers, though it works in other inkjet printers as well.

Every quilter who has worked with inkjet transfers has her own preferred brand of transfer paper which "works best." What works is really her particular combination of paper, printer, iron, etc. It may take many tests and trials to find the combination that gives you the most satisfying results. And since you are less likely to change computers or printers, trying various papers is one way to begin. Color preferences may also determine your satisfaction (or lack thereof) with particular combinations. I use red, magentas, and oranges a lot, so I want a paper/printer combination that gives me some degree of accuracy there. My friend, whose hands never touch reds, but who is pretty fanatical about blues and greens, has different criteria.

It is important to try papers from different manufacturers to find one that gives the most satisfactory results. Remember that a friend's preference for a specific paper may be partially influenced by her printer, fabric, and iron. One designer likes H-P transfers for their better color, though the "hand" is heavier. Another finds Epson to be heavier. They may not have started with fabrics of the same weight, which would affect the "hand" (as would fiber content).

Transfer sheets are constantly improving and changing. Newer ones are less stiff and more satisfactory than some of the earlier T-shirt transfers. They are more flexible and the hard shiny surface is gone.

HEAT TRANSFER SHEETS FOR INKJET PRINTERS

	Sources (by list number, see page 76)
Affinity Hot Peel and Cool Peel	(4, 8)
Epson Cool Peel	(5, 11)
Hanes T-Shirt Transfer	(4, 5, 13)
Hanes Easy Peel	(5, 13)
Jet-Wear!	(15)
Magic Transfer	(10)
Trans 4 Jet	(12)

Collaging

To make economical use of the photo transfer paper, place as many images on the scanner plate or the computer screen as will fit within the format of the print. This process can conserve transfer paper, but it may be time-consuming. The collage is then used to put the image on transfer paper.

GRANDMA'S WEDDING
by Diane E. Herbort, 16" x 20¼".
Photo by Diane E. Herbort.

This 1920s black-and-white wedding photo was first lightened, then printed with a mixture of red and black. The lettering was done on a computer and reversed for transfer. Diane used a cotton-linen setting to iron the transfer and added buttons and decorative details to cover damage and stains on the old lace.

GRANDMA'S 100TH BIRTHDAY QUILT
by Martie Carroll, 44" x 36".

Black-and-white photos were scanned into the computer, printed on inkjet transfer paper, and ironed onto 100% white cotton for this softly colored quilt. Martie used her hand painted fabrics and silk screen prints (with Thermofax) to complete the top. It is machine quilted with a complex pattern of stitches directly over the photo prints.

THE SIGN OF THE TRIANGLE
by Lisa Gray Hollerbach, 29" x 25".

Using an inkjet printer and TR-101 transfer sheets, Lisa transferred photos of her sons onto 100% cotton fabric for this panel. Also depicted are their Karate instructor and class photos. Lisa pieced and appliquéd both full-sized and trimmed photos. The student creed is printed on alternating blocks. Replicas of the traditional stitched belts are inserted at seamlines. Quilted into the background are many patterns and designs along with the words "black belt."

Detail of SEPT. 10, 1945 FIRST DAY OF SCHOOL
by Marsha Burdick. Photo by Marsha Burdick.

This charming photograph showing the quilter's first day at school was a black-and-white snapshot. After scanning it into her computer, she used Photoshop software to change it to a sepia-like color and enlarge it. When transferred to a finely woven cotton, it was hand painted to add color, giving an effect similar to hand-tinting. It is surrounded by forties fabrics in a log cabin assembly.

Printing the Image

Some computer printers require that sheets be inverted for printing—others accept them face up. Many papers (including TR-101, Jet-Ware, and Affinity's InkJet Print Media) are printed with green lines to identify the back of the page. Since this is a one-step process, the image will be reversed. If your computer has a reversal or mirror-image option, use that to correctly print the transfer. It will appear backwards until it is heat set. The transfers on fabric will be slightly tacky until they are dry, so avoid stacking them.

To print a photo onto a transfer sheet, you will need to scan the photo into the computer. If you don't have a scanner, some print shops will scan your photo and copy it to a disk. Make sure you have compatible software to open the file. Clip-art images are available for scanning and thousands of click-art images are available as software.

Hanes has T-shirt Maker software with ready-to-print graphics, but make sure it is compatible with your computer. They also sell their T-shirt transfer paper by the packet. It can be printed in the inkjet printer for transfer to cloth with an iron.

Heat Setting

A heat press will simplify home heat transferring since it will get hotter than an iron. It also applies pressure to the transfer, which helps set the polymer into the cloth. Use the press at 350 to 375 degrees.

Use a non-steam iron if you have one, since steam vents may interfere with even heating. I get excellent results with an old (non-steam) iron. If you must use a steam iron, move it around so that the holes are less likely to leave un-transferred areas. Use no steam for heat setting, since moisture will interfere with the transfer. Always give the cloth a final ironing before placing the transfer on top so that any moisture will be removed.

Heat Transfer for Inkjet Printers (Hot Peel)

Prewash the fabric to remove any fabric finishes. Trim away any excess photo transfer paper or unneeded background, leaving only the image.

Some old irons will attain a higher temperature than new ones, but always use the highest setting (cotton or cotton/linen). I have a garage sale iron that has a flat sole plate, is heavy, and gets extremely hot.

Use a solid and lightly padded ironing surface. An ironing board is not sturdy enough. Use a board (a bread board will do), pad or cover it (a double-folded pillow case is adequate), and place it on a counter or a solid table. You may want to use a Teflon coated pressing cloth on the board (and under the transfer) with the Teflon side up to capture all reflected heat.

WHAT YOU NEED

- *Iron and board*
- *Vinegar rinse*

STEPS

1. *Preheat fabric by ironing to remove any moisture.*
2. *Place transfer paper face down on fabric.*
3. *Heat set each area for 20 to 30 seconds. Peel paper as per directions.*
4. *Let dry (2 to 24 hours) and use vinegar rinse if required (see below).*

☞ TROUBLESHOOTING FOR TRANSFER SHEETS FOR INKJET PRINTERS

PROBLEM: *Image is cracked or crazed.*
SOLUTION: *Use a lower heat setting or iron for a shorter amount of time.*

PROBLEM: *Prints are spotty, cloudy, or unevenly transferred.*
SOLUTION: *Use higher heat and more pressure, holding the iron in each spot for about 20 seconds.*

PROBLEM: *Image is distorted or stretched.*
SOLUTION: *Pull from top, not diagonally. Have someone hold the fabric down while you remove the paper.*

PROBLEM: *Parts of the image remain on the transfer sheet.*
SOLUTION: *Remove paper slowly so that if a transfer is incomplete you can replace the transfer paper and add more heat.*

PROBLEM: *Blurry, fuzzy edges or loss of definition.*
SOLUTION: *In the print quality option, select economy or draft instead of best.*

Vinegar Rinse

Use a vinegar rinse on all heat set inkjet transfers to maximize color retention. Canon's TR-101, Affinity cool peel, and TMT Jet-Wear! require the vinegar as a pre-wash. For the rinse add one cup of white distilled vinegar to a low level of cold water in your washing machine. Put the fabric transfer into this vinegar water and complete the washing cycle on cool. Remove fabric immediately and dry under normal settings.

If you are printing T-shirts, this vinegar step is very important because T-shirts go through the laundry so often. I'm personally not greatly concerned about washing my pieces (primarily wallhangings), but for anything that might occasionally be washed, I use the vinegar rinse anyway. But then I stop at stop signs even if nobody else is at the intersection.

Care

If a transferred fabric needs to be laundered (assuming you used the vinegar rinse), wash gently in cool water and air dry or lay flat to dry. On subsequent washings, use cool water, detergent with color protection, and no bleach. I'd avoid all detergent and Woolite (which removes color from some prints). Orvus paste or soap is safer.

Avoid setting a hot iron directly on the area of transfer. If pressing is necessary, first cover the transfer with a Teflon coated cloth or a sheet of paper.

Printing Directly Onto Fabric

We'd all like to print directly on our fabrics and have the images be permanent, but until permanent inks replace soluable inks in inkjets, here are some alternatives:

1. Heat transfer papers for inkjet
2. Canon fabric sheets, Dharma's inkjet silk sheets
3. Spray finishes, mordants, and fabric treatments for printing directly on fabric

Canon Fabric Sheets FS-101 (for Canon Bubble Jet Computer Printers)

This printer-ready package consists of a piece of white fabric attached to a clear acetate backing. It was designed for direct printing to fabric on the Canon Bubble Jet printer.

The strips of adhesive on the transparent acetate backing (to which the fabric is adhered) align with the feeders in Canon printers, but when used in other printers, the strips may cause the fabric to be pulled from the backing, rendering a misprint. When the fabric is removed from the plastic backing and reapplied to freezer paper, it works great. Since no heat is generated in inkjet printers, neither the adhesive strips nor the plastic of the freezer paper pose a problem. These sheets are thicker than ordinary papers so you may have to adjust the printer to accommodate them. Some printers have a fabric sheet setting, others a coated paper option. Otherwise, adjust the thickness lever, or use the envelope option.

These fabric sheets come with a packet of Canon's "Colorfast" rinse. I found that even when that step was eliminated the image was vibrant and bright, and did not fade in a first hand-washing. The Colorfast fixative is designed to make colors less subject to fading, and since its use is recommended by the manufacturer it's probably a good idea.

The fabric is apparently permeated with a mordant, which makes it receptive to the inks, though Canon would not (of course!) tell me what it was. Another person answering my call assured me that there was no treatment or mordant on the fabric. However, even when I eliminated the Colorfast rinse step, the colors did not immediately wash out, so obviously this is not just an ordinary piece of fabric.

Because Canon Fabric Sheets are more expensive than heat transfer sheets, there are few sources for them (other than direct from Canon). However, as more people use them with great results the increased demand will lead to better availability.

Some quilt or fabric shops carry packets of fabric (pink, beige, and white), already adhered to freezer paper, called Computer Printer Fabric. I was pretty excited to see these, assuming they were similar to Canon Fabric Sheets. But they are just freezer paper on cloth and are not treated in any way. When printed, they offer no degree of permanence and cannot be washed (they'd be fine for embroidery patterns). It is true that they can go through your computer printer, but so can any fabric to which you add the paper backing. At $8 for a packet of four sheets that's pretty pricey. I discovered the "do not wash" in very small print on the back of the packet, and no address or phone number is given.

Always read labels and directions on any product you purchase. And make sure there is a phone number you can call for help and information.

CANON FABRIC SHEETS
(9 ½" X 14")

	Sources (by list number, see page 76)
Canon Fabric Sheets	(4, 5, 7)

———— **WHAT YOU NEED** ————

• *Computer lettering or artwork, or scanned image*

• *Canon Fabric Sheet FS-101*

• *Inkjet printer*

• *Iron and board*

• *(Freezer paper if you are not using a Canon printer)*

———— **THE PROCESS** ————

1 *For a non-Canon printer, remove plastic backing from cloth, press freezer paper to cloth and cut to fit, trimming edges carefully.*

2 *Adjust printer paper size to 9 ½" x 14".*

3 *Place one sheet of fabric in tray.*

4 *Print the image.*

5 *Peel fabric from backing.*

6 *Rinse in Canon's Colorfast solution, following the directions, and dry thoroughly.*

7 *Cover with paper and press.*

After printing on your fabric sheet, simply peel the fabric from the transparent backing (or the freezer paper). A packet of Colorfast (provided with the fabric sheet) is used for the rinse, then the print is dried and ironed. Results are permanent and vibrant. Be careful not to breathe dust from the packet of rinse.

☛ **TROUBLESHOOTING FOR CANON FABRIC SHEETS**

PROBLEM: *Misprint. Fabric sheet pulls or folds and does not feed smoothly.*

SOLUTION: *Eliminate the clear backing sheet and stabilize the fabric with freezer paper.*

PROBLEM: *Spots or specks appear on the print.*

SOLUTION: *There may be lint, dust specks, or threads on the cloth, on the scanner, or in the printer.*

PROBLEM: *Colors are not true.*

SOLUTION: *Adjust colors on computer software. This is a problem of the printer's inaccurate translation of colors from your computer, not a fabric sheet problem.*

Many artists have worked extensively with the Canon Fabric Sheets.

As well, Dharma's new silk fabric sheets should be available by the time this book is published. These are sheets prepared for inkjet printing and which require a spray, followed by a steam bath, to make the prints permanent.

Spray Finishes, Fixatives, and Mordants for Printing Directly on Fabric

	Sources (by list number, see page 76)
Fixatives	(2)
Transfer sheets	(1, 4)
Mending tape	(3)
Deka-Print Colorless Textile Screening Ink	(2, 9)
Synthrapol	(10)
Retayne	(10, 14)
Soda ash	(10, 14)
Deka Series L Textile Dye Fixative	(9)

Quilters have experimented with just about everything in their attempts to make inkjet prints on cloth impervious to water. Several of these methods require that the fabric be stabilized by adhering to freezer paper. Directions for this relatively simple process follow.

Using Stabilized Fabric for Inkjet Prints

Since fabrics are too soft and flexible to feed through the printer, they must first be stabilized if you want to print directly onto fabric.

Cut the freezer paper to the exact size you will feed into your printer (8.5" x 11", 8.5" x 14", etc.). Use a finely woven (200 thread count), white or light colored cotton fabric. Press it and place the freezer paper face down on top, the edge of the paper aligned with the grain of the fabric. Heat set with a medium-hot iron until the two are bonded. With too little heat, edges may be loose. With too much heat, it will be difficult to peel the two apart. Trim fabric to the exact size of paper. Leave no loose threads. These laminated fabrics will sometimes curl toward the fabric but can be flattened by running the iron over the paper side.

A stabilized fabric printed in an inkjet produces vivid images that run or bleed when wet and almost disappear entirely in washing. To make these prints more stable, quilters have devised various methods and recipes.

Fixative

Spraying a fixative over an inkjet print on stabilized fabric will help set the color on the fabric. Among the brands preferred by fiber artists are Krylon Workable Fixatif, Grumbacher, and Blair Spray-Fix. These measures help but do not entirely solve the problem. The hand of the fabric is changed, leaving it a little less soft and flexible. The sprays also tend to make the colors run, so they must be used very cautiously. A very light initial coating, once dry, can be safely covered with subsequent sprays.

A major concern with spray finishes is the potential harm from vapors. Spray out of doors or with good ventilation and wear a paper mask (such as painters use). Use special caution if you make extensive use of the fixatives.

MT. RAINIER
by Marjorie Horton, 15½ x 21½. Image by Martie Carroll.
Marjorie scanned her photo of Mt. Rainier, then manipulated the colors digitally before printing the image on transfer paper in her inkjet printer. Quilting lines follow the image. The border, which was pieced in a perspective pattern, was inspired by Angela Madden, the British author of *Pieceful Scenes*.

TUSCANY
by Becky Sundquist, 44" x 60". Photo by Don Tuttle.

Of the thirteen different images used to compose this quilt, those of the wine country were scanned into the computer while the others were fed directly into the computer from video. All were Becky's own photographs. After printing her images directly to cloth in the inkjet printer, she fixed the color by heat setting blank Magic Transfer papers over them, using a home heat press. She used a CAD (computer aided drafting) program along with Photoshop to create the various parts, which she then appliquéd. She enhanced the prints with ink, markers, and paint, adding embroidery and both machine and hand stitching.

COME BACK SHAINA
by Bonnie Askowitz, 16" x 24".
Images by Sharon T. Rothberg.
Photo by Daniel Arsenio Oria.

The artist scanned photographs of her daughter and granddaughter, then modified them on her computer for this series of wall quilts. After she made her transfers to fabric, Bonnie used a single coat of brown Deka Fabric paint to relate the fabric colors to the images. She protected the transfers with muslin in order to heat set the paint.

Transfer Sealant

Another method for making the jet prints more permanent involves the use of heat transfers (for CLC or inkjet) to seal or fix the ink to the cloth. Stabilize the fabric, print it, then remove the freezer paper. Let the printed image dry, then heat set it. Place an unprinted sheet of inkjet transfer paper, cut to cover the image, with the polymer side face-to-face with the image. Heat transfer, then rinse in a diluted vinegar solution. The polymer serves as a fixative which coats the fabric and gives it a damp look, a slight sheen, and some degree of permanency. This will give a slight stiffness and much the same look as if you printed on the transfer sheet initially.

Becky Sundquist (quilt page 35) uses this method to fix her inkjet prints. After heat setting with a home press, she sets the fabric a second time using a photo transfer sheet and a Teflon cloth. This helps the coating soak into the fabric, giving it a better hand.

Mending Tape

Once the stabilized fabric has been printed, remove the freezer paper. Then use mending tape to coat inks that are not permanent. Heat set the tape to the image and peel away while it is still hot. Should it be necessary to overlap the mending tape, overlapping edges will not show. It may be easier and faster to use transfer paper, however, and probably less expensive for full-size sheets. As well, Gail Chase reported that Bondex over TR-101 made the ink run, though another designer used the same combination successfully.

Extender Base

Some quilters treat cloth they have printed in the inkjet by coating it with the extender base used for silk screen printing (Deka-Print Colorless Textile Screening Ink, for example). This is an extender for water-based ink which becomes impervious to water once it has dried or set. Other extenders for water-based textile inks work similarly: Versatex, Delta, or Speedball for example.

Luanne Cohen has developed a method for applying extender base using a silk screen frame and squeegee. Allow the transferred image to set for a few hours before removing the stabilized fabric from its paper backing, place a silk screen frame down on top of it. The screen must be as large as the inkjet image. Add the extender base at one end of the screen, then use the squeegee in a single stroke to apply it. Immediately lift the screen, remove the paper and hang to dry. Iron, image side down, for 30 seconds using cotton/linen setting.

The extender (sometimes called transparent base) can be brushed on right from the container but care must be taken or the colors will spread. The fabric must be stabilized before printing and the freezer paper backing can be left in place during brushing.

Fabric Softener

Pre-washing your fabric in a fabric softener makes it somewhat more receptive to the inkjet ink, depending on what ink your printer uses. The combination of additive-free fabric softener and a fixative improves color retention. It will not make the print permanent, however.

Mordant

On the internet you'll find various recipes to help make the inkjet prints on cloth more permanent. Some recommend the use of Synthrapol, which is a pre-rinse designed to remove impurities that may interfere with dyes. It also keeps any excess dye particles in suspension to prevent them from adding color where it is not wanted. It is used at a ratio of ¼ cup per washer load.

Another product that several people recommend is Retayne, a rinse that prevents color bleeding during washing. It is used one teaspoon per yard in hot water. Both of these mordants are used before the fabric is stabilized.

Combination Treatment to Prepare Fabric For Printing Directly on Cloth with the Inkjet Printer

Melissa Boyd has developed a way to make her inkjet prints somewhat washfast. She finds that it does take time but will extend a limited budget. After following her directions the fabrics can sustain numerous hand washings (or one or two machine washings).

1. Soak fabric for 15 minutes in a solution of ½ water and ½ Downy Ultra Free softener.

2. Rinse for 20-30 seconds, line dry, and iron flat.

3. Heat set freezer paper to fabric, trim to size, and spray with Static Guard (or other anti-static spray). Dry completely.

4. Print fabric in an inkjet printer, setting the paper thickness lever to maximum (or use the transparency mode). Place only one sheet at a time in the tray.

5. Spray the color print with an artist's fixative.

Melissa says that each of steps 1, 3, and 5 improve washability. Use all three for maximum effectiveness. After trying sixteen different clear coatings, she found these to be most effective: Blair Matte Spray Fix, Krylon Workable Fixatif #1306, or Deft Semi-Gloss Clear Wood Finish (in spray can). Her experiments were done on various models of HP printers, so test your samples first. Then iron with a cool iron.

The fabric softener and anti-static spray contain chemical salts that bind to the fibers as well as to the inkjet inks. The fixative physically bonds the dyes to the fabric and will stiffen it somewhat. Avoid touching the fixative-coated fabric with a hot iron as it may discolor.

Another good recipe appears in *The Quilter's Computer Companion*, where authors Judy Heim and Gloria Hansen offer the results of their extensive testing in search of an effective fixative for inkjet prints.

☞ **TROUBLESHOOTING FOR SPRAY FINISHES, MORDANTS, AND OTHER FINISHES**

PROBLEM: *Colors faded when the fixative-coated cloth was washed.*

SOLUTION:: *Use a light initial spray followed by a heavier one. Several additional coats of fixative may be necessary.*

PROBLEM: *Transfer sheet stiffens the fabric.*

SOLUTION: *Heat set it several times, until the transfer soaks into fabric. There will always be some change in the "hand" of the fabric, but pressing helps.*

PROBLEM: *Mending tape didn't peel off the inkjet printed fabric.*

SOLUTION: *Re-heat the tape and remove it while it's hot. Cover any exposed areas of transfer with paper.*

PROBLEM: *Spots or specks appear on the print.*

SOLUTION: *Clean all copy and fabric surfaces so they are free of lint, threads, and dust. Be sure the print on cloth is clear before covering it with protective coating.*

PROBLEM: *Printed fabric runs when washed, despite mordant.*

SOLUTION: *Give fabric a longer soaking in mordant, use more fixative.*

No Scanner? Other Computer Possibilities

If you don't have a scanner but do have a computer and black-and-white printer, you have several options:

• Enter words, names, or other text and then select from a range of fonts and sizes to print these out. If you have a black-and-white printer, print your words and add color in almost any way (marking pen, crayon, colored pencils, acrylics, etc.). Take your text to a copy shop, run it through a CLC, adjust or add color, and copy it to transfer paper.

• Use click art or copyright-free images (software available on diskette or CD) to print images in the same way.

• Use a drawing program to create your artwork, do a print-out, add color, then take your print-out to a copy shop and have it copied on a CLC onto transfer paper.

• Print directly onto freezer paper backed fabric, then protect the surface as described under Spray Finishes, Fixatives, and Mordants, page 32-36. See *Imagery on Fabric* for more details on this process.

CHAPTER 4
family quilts

Everybody has at least one cherished photo brimming with sentimental meaning or chock full of personal significance. With their silent appeal, these photos invite us to create nostalgic quilts and panels—soft memories. Who doesn't love seeing their great-grand-mother's portrait permanently displayed on a pillow or a wallhanging?

Memories given visible form are heart-warming keepsakes. Some recollection quilts are organized around an event, such as a wedding or a family reunion. Others commemorate teams, classes, clubs,

or guilds. Sometimes an occurrence, such as the Hale-Bopp comet, the launching of the Hubble telescope, or a birthday, provides the idea, or a stack of photos and snapshots of a single person may comprise an entire quilt.

Many first photo transfer quilts are album-like, with photos aligned in rows. Recording the photos on cloth is the primary concern. Familiarity with the process allows the development of an individual approach.

WHEN THEY WERE YOUNG
by Jan Krentz, 33" x 42 ½".
   For this Storm at Sea quilt, Jan used decorative "corner cropping" scissors to impart a photo album look. She prefers to have a copy shop do all her heat transfers since she finds she cannot get adequate pressure or heat on her home iron.

STARS OF THE FAMILY.
by Jan Krentz. 22½" x 22½".

Color photo transfers form parts of the "stars" in this quilt.
Each star was individually drawn on a six-inch piece of freezer paper. The stars were deliberately cut in random sizes
with points shifting as needed to accommodate the transfers.
Some photo backgrounds were cut away and the figures
were appliquéd. Others are reverse appliqué or raw edge
appliqué.

WEDDING PLACEMATS
by Martie Carroll, each 11" x 18". Photo by Martie Carroll.

A set of four placemats, two of which are shown here, celebrates a sister's family with old and new photos in both black-and-white and color. Some transfers were copied onto Photo Effects; others were on Kinko's paper (which Martie prefers). All transfers were heat set at home using an iron. The mats are finished with free-motion quilting in metallic threads.

Details of FORGET ME NOT
by Diane Herbort.

Vintage postcards (circa 1910) and valentines were used in these nostalgic collages. Photo Textiles made the transfers, adjusting the color to compensate for the yellowing of the cards. Laces and edgings cover the edges of the transfers in this crazy-pieced panel, pieced by machine and by hand.

MILLS FAMILY REUNION QUILT
by Jan Hirth, 30" x 32".

At the Mills family reunion, fifteen adults and four kids made photo quilts. Each family contributed one photo, which was copied fifteen times in 3½" squares, six to each page of transfer paper. With four different brands of transfer paper at hand they soon became expert with the iron-on process. Inexperienced quilters were paired with those more experienced and in five days almost all the quilts were finished!

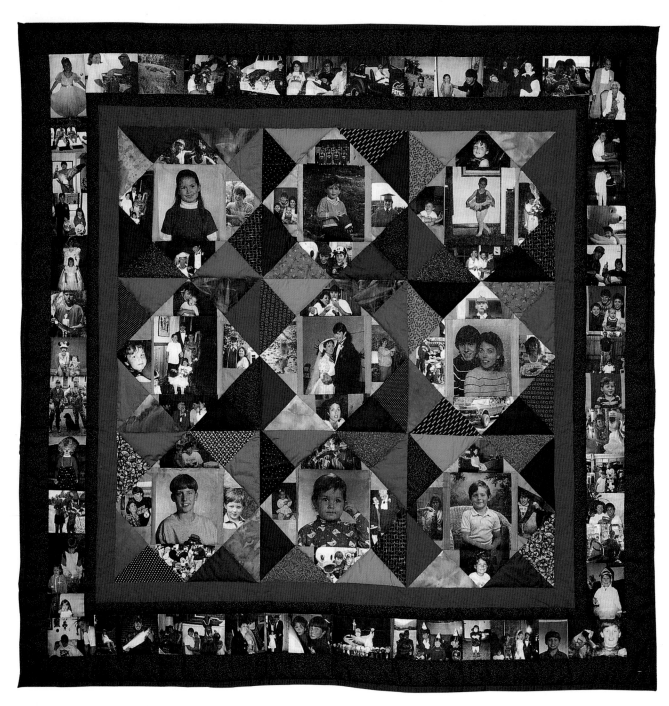

DAVID'S FAMILY
by Jackie Vermeer, 51½" x 51½".

Photos of every size appear in this vivid and lively collection. Larger photos, all squares of about the same size, were used for the central blocks. If a rectangular photo couldn't be trimmed square, Jackie made it square by adding green or blue paper before copying to transfer paper. Smaller snapshots were used in the triangles. All the hand quilting was "in the ditch" to avoid sewing through the transfers. The border, too, is packed with snapshots. For all these transfers, Jackie used One Step paper and a hand iron.

Mobilgas logo used with permission of Mobil Oil Corporation.

TROPHIES
by Sue Pierce, 46" x 46".

Sue Pierce's tribute to her father commemorates his life, death, and battle with Alzheimer's disease. The chronologically arranged game board includes a report card, college diploma, photos of first child and first house, and so on. She used transfer paper from Ami Simms, had them copied on a CLC, and transferred them at home with an iron.

SARAH: JOURNALS AND POEMS
by Bonnie Peterson, 35" x 38". Photo by Bonnie
Peterson.

    Single panels, each edged and hemmed in
black fabric, are joined together by loops. Each
section started as a piece of batting to which Bonnie bonded interfacing to stiffen it. Rayon and
polyester fabrics were bonded to the surface next,
and then her journals were photo transferred over
that. On the reverse of each unit are poems painted
with air pens from Silk Paint Corp.

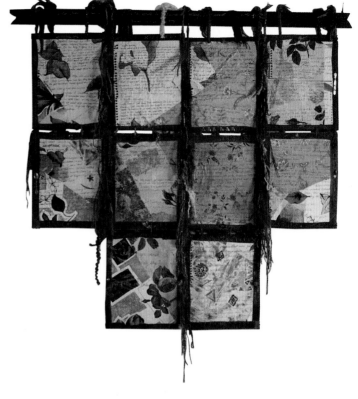

TREASURED MEMORIES
by Jan Krentz, 47½ x 61".

    After lightening and balancing some of the colors
in the CLC, Jan had her photos copied onto transfer
paper. She then cut the ovals before heat transferring
them to cloth. The four-point stars were set into a
variation of Storm at Sea, which accommodated both
vertical and horizontal photos.

DREAM HOUSE
by Kristin Otte, 36" x 38".

Diplomas, certificates, report cards, envelopes, newspaper announcements, and photos fill Kristin's quilt. She used a variety of photo transfer methods, including several made with mending tape. All are on sateen. The gray range of the lightened copies blends with the off-white and pastel fabrics. Free-motion quilting created wavy lines over the entire surface.

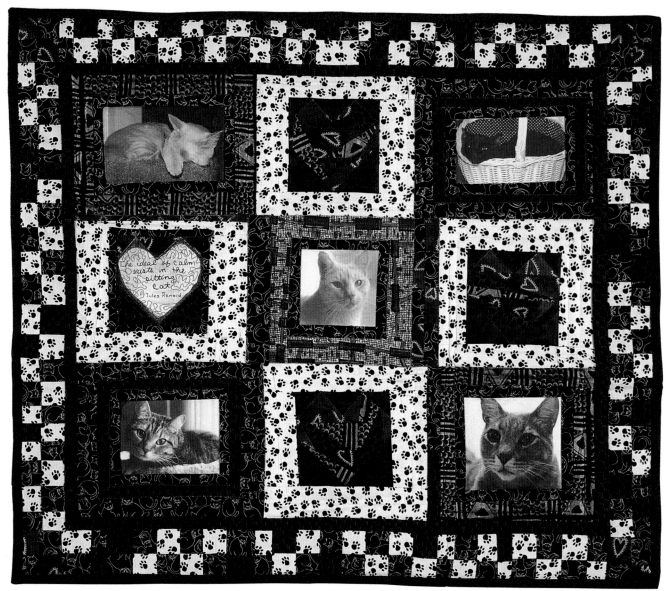

FOR GARTH, MAGGIE, SAM & ELIOT
by Sharon L. Benton, 24" x 26".

After photographing her cats, both wide-eyed and sleep-ing, Sharon color-adjusted the 35mm film images on the CLC. The central cat (which was bluish) was altered by adding yellow and removing cyan, and the background was deliberately blurred or smudged to emphasize the foreground. The photos were copied to transfer paper at a copy shop and heat set at home. With a modified square-in-a-square to frame each cat, Sharon created crazy-pieced hearts.

SCOUTING RUNS IN FAMILIES
by Marsha Burdick, 13" x 14".

Three photos of different sizes were each enlarged with strips of fabric until they fit together into a rectangle for this pillow.

FRANCE
by Bonnie Peterson, 43" x 54". Photo by Bonnie Peterson.
   Over transferred maps of France, Bonnie added the heads of sixty French and American children who participated in an exchange program. Other images include the Statue of Liberty, newspaper items, airline images from travel brochures, and other memorabilia. She first transferred the images to cloth and then added Wonder-Under to the entire 11" x 17". The order of these steps is important since the transfers require greater heat than the fabric adhesive.

Detail of FRANCE
by Bonnie Peterson. Photo by Bonnie Peterson.
Once her transfers were backed with Wonder-Under, Bonnie cut them out and applied them individually to the panel, peeling the paper away last. The quilt was a gift to the French school from the American kids who went there.

THE RAIN FELL DOWN
by Kathleen Deneris, 55" x 28".

Katie, Ali, Sam, and Olivia did their high-spirited paintings using poster paints. Kathleen took these to a Kinko's Copy Shop where they reduced and duplicated the images before copying them onto transfer paper. She transferred them at home using a press (cotton setting for two minutes). The "rain" is machine quilted over the assembled parts. A composite transfer photo of the young artists was machine appliquéd to the back (see photo page 16) and sewing-machine script creates the label.

VALENTINE and HAPPY VALENTINE'S DAY, PETER
by Judith Wagstrom, each 9" x 7½".

The soft effect in the valentines results from the use of silk organza used over the photo transfers. In Peter's valentine, a heart is placed over the figure and cut to fit the hand shape, so the hands appear to be holding the heart. The photo is printed in its original black and white. Sequins, beads, and stamp prints are added.

THE HOUSE THAT MAX BUILT
by Kathleen Deneris, 48" x 36".

   A child's drawings made with Crayola Color Change
markers on paper were the originals for this quilt. Kathleen
had the drawings reduced to varying sizes and then printed
onto transfer paper at Kinko's Copy Shop. The drawings were
elaborated with machine quilting in multiple colors, applied
with the same exuberance and activity as that used in the
drawings and the printed borders. The child's photo was transferred to the back of the quilt.

TIME TO SMELL THE FLOWERS
by Lilly Thorne, 42" x 58".

After enlarging and reducing her photos, Lilly copied them onto transfer paper at a copy shop and heat pressed them to cloth at home using an Elna press. Lilly combined her hand-dyed fabrics with the transfers, a process she teaches in British Columbia, Canada. Photos include those of six children (his, hers, and theirs) along with shots of flowers, trees, and clouds.

CHAPTER 5
Clothing

Few things are more fun to wear than the clothes to which you have added transfers. Anyone who has enjoyed a T-shirt with the image of Beethoven or Einstein will love the possibility of adding a significant other—a special cat or a favorite niece—to her wardrobe.

Because transfers add body, or a slight stiffness, to the fabric, they should be used judiciously on garments. Seams which run through the transfers add further stiffness, so cut away any excess parts of the transfer paper before heat setting to the fabric. There are some portions of a garment where extra body may be desirable, so try to transfer to those areas—cuffs, for example, belts, or the straight-cut front of a boxy jacket. Transfers to yokes or backs are more easily worn than those that come at a waistline, where they will be tucked in. They would be less appropriately used on soft fabrics or on those that drape. However, as new and improved papers continue to appear on the market, perhaps they'll soon be flexible enough to use on any weight of cloth.

One means of reducing the area of transfer (and thus any stiffness) is by cutting away all extraneous material before transferring the image to cloth, leaving a silhouetted form. The plain background of the fabric is preferable to the telephone poles, buildings, or cars that occasionally appear in the backgrounds of snapshots. You will also limit the amount of unnecessary stiffness by using small images. For example, use images just 1" to 2" high on socks, hankies, kids' shirts, pajamas, or shorts.

Using ready-made articles or garments allows additional play time that would otherwise go into clothing construction. The most popular are T-shirts, sweatshirts, boxer shorts, dish towels, scarves, and totes. Unlined cotton blazers are great. If the fiber content of the pre-made piece will not tolerate high heat, transfer to cotton fabric which can then be appliquéd to your garment.

NEW ZEALAND VESTS
by Beverly Erickson.
   At a copy shop, Beverly transferred photos of a trip to New Zealand to cloth. Next she arranged the trimmed transfers on the white fabric vest parts. She lightly sprinkled Astonish (a bonding powder) on the moistened perimeter of the back of each transfer. To protect the transfers while she heat set the bonding powder, Beverly covered them with a silicon cloth. Trims, braids, and ribbons were bonded or stitched over all raw edges, then the vest parts were assembled.

RETIREMENT VEST
by Beverly Erickson.
   A ready-made twill vest provided the base for this collection of photos. Each photo was transferred to white fabric, cut and adhered with Astonish to the beige vest, then machine stitched at the outer edge. The vest offers a moving photo album of a retirement trip.

Front of HELLO FRIEND, BILL COSBY VEST
by Kata Patton.

Excited over the prospects of Bill Cosby's upcoming performance in her home town, Kata made a special vest for the occasion. Not only did Cosby sign a fabric for the vest (he thought she was "super fantastically great" for having the courage to put his face on it) but the local TV station's film of her wearing it was aired just before an interview with him. Kata used a local shop to have the transfer made and ironed it on at home. The back of Kata's vest includes Jell-O's original packaging and Mr. Cosby's signature and photo.

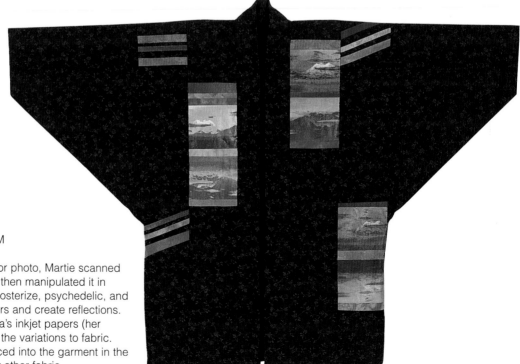

Front of MT. RAINIER AT 2 AM
by Martie Carroll.

Working from a 35mm color photo, Martie scanned the image into her computer, then manipulated it in Corel Photo-Paint using the posterize, psychedelic, and inversion options to alter colors and create reflections. After printing them on Dharma's inkjet papers (her favorite) she heat transferred the variations to fabric. These were inserted and pieced into the garment in the same way she would use any other fabric.

Front of WESTERN JACKET
by Louise Thompson.

Western fabric used to line this jacket also provided the images for the decorative details. The cowboy border was copied onto Xerox transfer paper, then home ironed onto Ultrasuede. Louise's hand-dyed fabrics, alternated with checkerboard fabrics, provide the body of this suede-fringed jacket.

Back detail of WESTERN JACKET
by Louise Thompson.

Two transfers aligned end-to-end make a perfect match of the border print on the yoke of this western jacket.

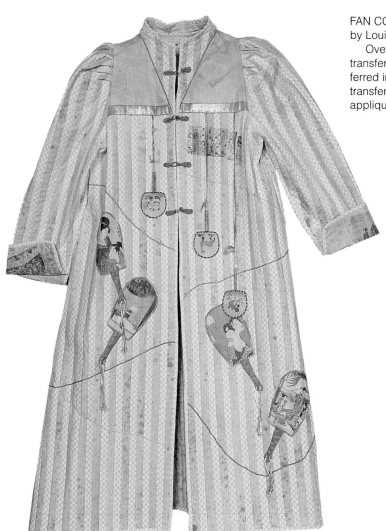

FAN COAT
by Louise Thompson.

Over the strip-pieced body of this coat, Louise added transfers in two different ways. At upper right, she transferred images from old postcards. The large fans were photo transferred to white fabric, cut into fan shapes, and machine appliquéd to the coat.

Detail of FAN COAT
by Louise Thompson.

After hanging fabric over the back fence, Louise threw paint at it to create an all-over spatter texture. She then alternated strips of the spatter fabric with white-on-white checks to form the base of this coat. Cuffs have transfers on both front and back.

DAVID'S STATS
by Marsha Burdick.

A black-and-white hospital photo (5" x 7") and footprint were scanned into a Macintosh computer. Marsha used Photoshop software to add some aqua color to the black tones and Canvas software to include David's birth statistics. The panel of stats includes the birth weight and height as well as the current weight and height of the quilter's now 40-year-old son. Perhaps the only thing missing is his current footprint.

CHAPTER 6

Studio Quilts

Panels, wallhangings, and quilts made with photo transfer are as varied as the quilters themselves. It is the experimental and inventive designers who point out new ways of working and who coax the artistic worlds of wonder out of these plastic-coated sheets of paper.

Most of the pieces in this section are works that will be hung on the wall, so added body (or change of the fabric's "hand") and washability are not necessarily a consideration. One characteristic of these artists'

works is that their transfers become an integral part of an overall idea. The transfers are not an end in themselves, but make up the elements of their compositions.

Many use transfers as they would any other printed fabric, incorporating the patterns and shapes into their designs. Here, however, designers have the advantage of creating their own patterns or images on the cloth. These works are unique, personal, and exciting. All find and stretch the limits of new ways to use photo transfer.

URBAN FLIGHT
by Deborah Melton Anderson, 27" x 31". Photo by Carina Woolrich. Image by J. Kevin Fitzsimons.

Working on a single piece of white cotton fabric, Deborah transferred 3" x 3" units, each with a half-inch drop at one edge. The birds were created by tucking the fabric in back before ironing on the transfers. She takes her own photos on a point-and-shoot Nikon, and in this piece captured distorted views of buildings from which she created her image of the city as a giant aviary. This remarkable work depicts parts of San Francisco, Chicago, Istanbul, and Athens.

HANDEL AT WORK AND PLAY
by Wendy Huhn, 46" x 35"

As one of ten artists selected to create a cover for the Oregon Symphony program guides, Wendy was given Handel as her composer for the month of December. She used CLC for the images of animals, cherubs, angels, and Handel, which she glued to the surface of the panel using Weld-Bond, a PVC glue. The orchestra was stenciled.

A BETTER BRONX
by Sandra Sider, 28" x 76". Photo by Sandra Sider.

Installed on a convex curving wall, this large piece (one of a series of commissions for a hospital) consists primarily of photo transfers, all made at Photo Textiles. To accommodate the curve, Sandra used a collage technique, stitching one transfer over the edge of an adjoining one. The five photos used were all sites within a five minute walk of the clinic, and all contained windows or open areas. It was machine quilted over batting and embellished with hand embroidery.

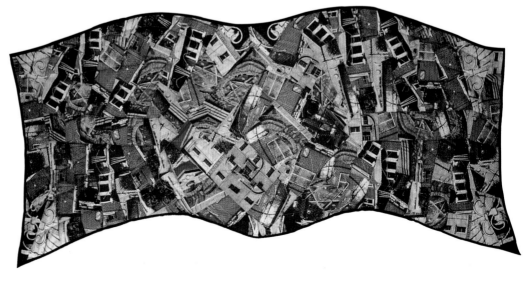

HOW I WON HIM BY A BLONDE
by Wendy Huhn, 28" x 37".
Photo by David L. Loveall.
This classic piece sheds new light on what fomented the Trojan War! Paris seems to have been influenced by the dazzling shoes and blonde tresses of Venus. Here, the goddesses not chosen carry hatchets and hard looks to express their displeasure. While their checkerboards are stenciled, all figures, lipsticks, foliage, and beauties of the natural world are photo transfers.

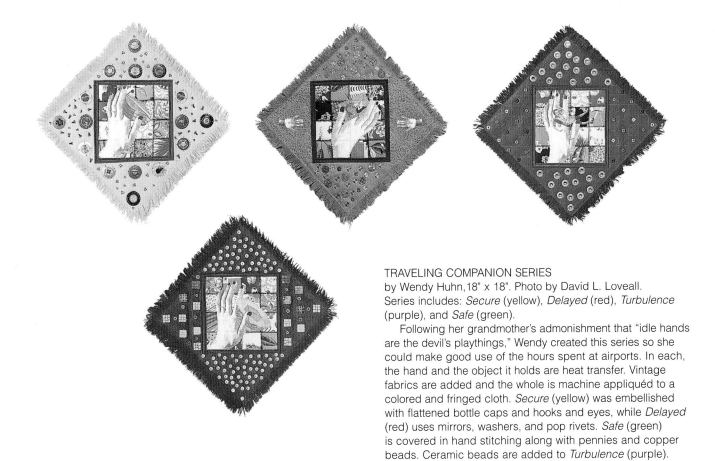

TRAVELING COMPANION SERIES
by Wendy Huhn, 18" x 18". Photo by David L. Loveall.
Series includes: *Secure* (yellow), *Delayed* (red), *Turbulence* (purple), and *Safe* (green).
Following her grandmother's admonishment that "idle hands are the devil's playthings," Wendy created this series so she could make good use of the hours spent at airports. In each, the hand and the object it holds are heat transfer. Vintage fabrics are added and the whole is machine appliquéd to a colored and fringed cloth. *Secure* (yellow) was embellished with flattened bottle caps and hooks and eyes, while *Delayed* (red) uses mirrors, washers, and pop rivets. *Safe* (green) is covered in hand stitching along with pennies and copper beads. Ceramic beads are added to *Turbulence* (purple).

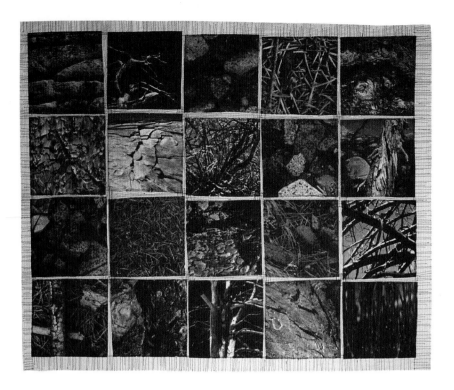

WALKING AWAY #1
by Bonnie Peterson, 27" x 33". Photo by
Bonnie Peterson.

While hiking through Yosemite National
Park as an artist in residence, Bonnie photographed what she saw at her feet. She
then copied her color prints on transfer
paper in black and white. Using her INSTA
T-shirt press, she transferred the images
to cloth. These were bonded with Wonder-
Under to another piece of white fabric, and
then machine stitching was added.

OLIVER'S BATTERY
by Sharon Doyle, 19½" x 28".
   A copy shop printed Sharon's 35mm slide onto Magic Touch transfer paper, then transferred it to cloth. She trimmed the white edges to create a deckle effect. This transfer was then used within a fabric landscape made from the same picture. She dyed, discharged, and hand painted her fabrics. Flowers were cut from commercial fabrics and appliquéd, and the whole was embellished with embroidery markers and quilting.

ELECTRIC TREE
by Katie Pasquini Masopust, 48" x 36".
Photo by Hawthorne Studio.
   Photos of clouds, transferred to fabric, are interspersed with blues and violets of various patterns and textures to create glimpses of natural sky. After making her transfers, Katie sorts them into her light, medium, and dark stacks and uses them as though they were printed materials.

(opposite page)
WINTER WALK
by Deborah Melton Anderson, 25" x 20".
Photo by Deborah Melton Anderson.
This beautiful and intriguing piece uses a variation of a technique of the Wolof people in Senegal (described in The Dyer's Art by Jack Lenor Larsen, 1976, Van Nostrand Reinhold Co., page 18). Deborah cut long strips of cotton sateen into various widths, then braided them and heat set transfers to both sides. She unbraided, then re-braided strips, exposing more areas to transfer. Braids were opened and the lengths stitched to a foundation fabric. The next step was to cut the panel lengthwise, moving centers to the outside. She then snipped away portions or added new transfers as needed for the composition. The inspiration was a hike in January to the Hocking Hills through snow, cold, and ice.

CAMBRIA SEEKS THE LIGHT THROUGH YONDER
WINDOW
by Gail Chase, 18" x 22".
   Starting with her selected image, Gail had a copy
shop print several copies in each of several sizes.
She then cut a template from card stock and created
her design, collaging the color prints into the template.
The collage was then copied to transfer paper, set
to cloth, and assembled for quilting. In her photogra-
phy, Gail likes creating borders, and does that here by
cloning an inner image to use in an outer area.

BRIDAL VEIL MEADOW
by Norah Madigan McMeeking, 34" x 38". Image by
James Austin. Photo by Sharon Risedorph.
   Using two photos taken by her son, Norah over-
lapped and cropped them to get the composition she
wanted. She started the quilt in a class with Katie
Pasquini Masopust, and particularly liked the idea
of "hiding" photos in a landscape. Areas of rocks,
several trees, and parts of the mountain face are
photo transfer.

RITES OF PASSAGE
by Sandra Sider, 34" x 48". Photo by Sandra Sider.

Working with her own architectural photos, Sandra covered them with clear acrylic sheets and highlighted architectural details in magenta and yellow with film marking pens. The colored acrylic sheet was placed over the photo and offset slightly before copying to transfer paper. Short sections of bright ribbons, in reverse appliqué, add contrast with their sheen. The piece is attached to the canvas backing with French knots.

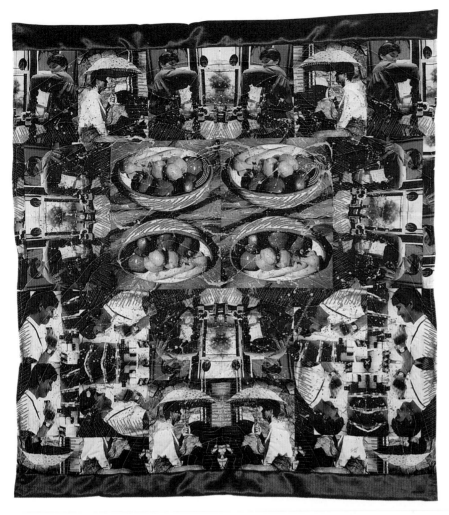

WOMEN AT WORK AND PLAY, NO. 6
by Sandra Sider, 48" x 44". Photo by
Sandra Sider.

The four portrait-studies (some mir-rored) were designed to reflect the incredi-ble energy and dedication of a nurse and friend. The fruit bowl (the fifth photo) and kitchen scene represent nurturing and shelter. The "work" was the hospital scene and the "play" was the friend's horsing around with the umbrella. Sandra worked on her color photos with a scalpel, to etch the emulsion, and with markers to add color in drawn lines.

LAST TOSS, COOBER PEDY
by Alvena B. Hall, 45" x 45".

If you saw *Priscilla, Queen of the Desert* you are familiar with Coober Pedy. It is in this remote desert opal-mining town that Alvena B. Hall, from South Australia, found inspiration for her quilt panel. She photographed an old car, abandoned on a mullock heap, as the central focus for her piece. This image showed her "dancing about madly in the moonlight, photographing amidst shards of broken glass." On the outside border, images of unending miles of desert as well as of the "dog fence" (to keep out the dingoes) were transferred full size from Xerox photocopies. Her use of fractured prints furthers the sense of the abandonment of discarded materials.

WOMEN AT WORK AND PLAY, NO. 8
by Sandra Sider, 52" x 32". Photo by Karen Bell.

    Using three photographs of her friend, Sandra had them mirror imaged and enlarged to about 8" x 12". After Photo Textiles transferred them to fabric for her, she colored some with diluted purple silk dye. The red stick shapes were made by placing a twig under the fabric and rubbing with crayon pastels. The "work" in the title refers to her friend's reading, the "play" to a swamp tour (thus the sawgrass). The historic architectural elements in the side borders are from a lamp post outside the New Orleans police station. This is the final in a series of eight wonderful panels.

THUNDEREGG CONCEPTION
by Pat White, 36" x 48".

Feeling a bit guilty when she hiked instead of pursuing her work, Pat found a way to combine the two. For this piece, she photographed the thundereggs (geodes, unique crystal centered volcanic rock formations) in the Yukon and combined them with her batiks and hand-dyed fabrics. She "got a little obsessed" and produced seventeen quilts for an exhibit to protest the selling of thundereggs to tourists.

QUEEN ANNE'S GARDEN
by Deborah Melton Anderson, 31" x 31". Image by J. Kevin
Fitzsimons. Photo by Deborah Melton Anderson.

The mandala aspect of this quilt results from Deborah's
work with the mirror-image capability of the CLC. Her photographs, taken primarily in Turkey, include scarves, flowers,
a fountain, and a stone carving. She transfers her images at
home using a home press.

Detail of QUEEN ANNE'S GARDEN
by Deborah Melton Anderson.
Photo by Deborah Melton Anderson.
Needle lace and beads enhance the already
intricate patterns of the Queen Anne's Lace.

CHAPTER 7

projects

Photo Pillow

PHOTO PILLOW
by Jean Ray Laury,
14" x 14".
   This pillow shows
inkjet transfers made from
a small snapshot that was
enlarged for use. It shows
an on-point variation of
the Square-In-A-Square
block.

Yardage and Cutting Requirements

Center: 4½" x 4½" white, finely-woven, 100% cotton
   fabric for photo transfer

Light Triangles: Two 3¾" x 3¾" squares of light-
   colored fabric, cut in half diagonally

Medium Triangles: Two 4⅞" x 4⅞" squares of
   medium-colored fabric, cut in half diagonally

Inner Border: Two 1½" x 8½" strips for the sides;
   two 1½" x 10½" strips for the top and bottom
   edges

Outer Border: Two 2¼" x 10½" strips for the sides;
   two strips 2¼" x 14" for the top and bottom
   edges

Pillow Back: Two 10" x 14" rectangles

Pillow Form: 14"

PILLOW CENTER

1. After enlarging or reducing your photograph as needed, transfer the image to fabric by the photo transfer method of your choice.

2. Using a ¼" seam allowance, follow the pillow construction illustration below. Sew a light-colored triangle to each edge of the photo square. Press seams toward the triangles.

3. Sew a medium-colored triangle to each edge of the resulting square. Press seams toward these triangles.

INNER BORDER

4. Sew the two 1½" x 8½" strips to the left and right edges of the square. Press. Sew the two 1½" x 10½" strips to the top and bottom edges. Press seams toward the border.

OUTER BORDER

5. Sew the two 2¼" x 10½" strips to the left and right edges of the square. Press. Sew the two 2¼" x 14" strips to the top and bottom edges. Press seams toward this border.

PILLOW FINISHING

6. Press under ¼" along one 14" edge of each pillow back piece. Press under another ¼" and topstitch this edge.

7. Overlap the folded edges of the two pieces, right sides up, to create a 14" square.

8. With right sides together, pin the pillow top and back together.

9. Sew around all four edges using a ½" seam allowance.

10. Turn right side out and insert the pillow form. The pillow form will fit snugly for a tight, puffy look.

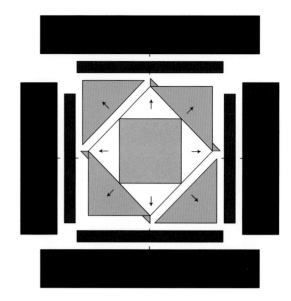

Pillow Construction

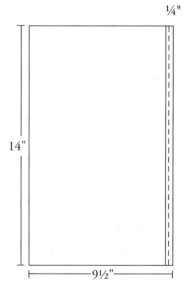

¼"

14"

9½"

Pillow Back - one side

Daniel

DANIEL
by Jan Krentz, 11½" x 18½".
    Jan transferred three photos featuring her son on his skateboard to a single piece of white fabric, with even spaces between them. Similar colors are reflected in the borders of the panel.

Yardage Requirements

Center: 7" x 14" white, finely-woven, 100% cotton fabric for photo transfer
Border: ⅛ yard each of three different plaid flannels
Border Corners: ⅛ yard polka-dot flannel
Backing: 13" x 19½"
Binding: ⅛ yard
Batting: 15" x 21½"

QUILT CENTER

1. After enlarging or reducing your photographs as needed, transfer to fabric, three 4" x 6" images by the photo transfer method of your choice. Leave ½" of space between the images and a ½" border all the way around.

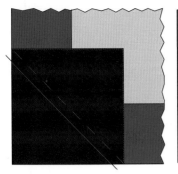
Sew and trim

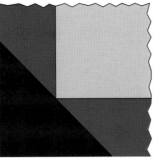
Press

BORDERS

2. For the border corners, cut twelve squares 2" x 2".

3. Cut two strips 1¼" x 14" from the first border fabric. Sew to the top and bottom edges of the quilt top. Cut two strips 1¼" x 8½". Sew to the left and right edges.

4. Lay a border corner square on a border corner, matching the corners, and stitch from corner to corner. Press. Trim excess plaid fabric from underneath border corner. Repeat for the other three corners.

5. To add the second border, measure the quilt from side to side across the center. Cut two strips 1¼" by this measurement. Sew to the top and bottom edges of the quilt top. Measure the quilt from top to bottom across the center including the borders you have just added. Cut two strips 1¼" by this measurement. Sew to the left and right edges.

6. Add the border corners as in step 4.

7. Repeat steps 5 and 6 to add the third border and border corners.

8. Press the quilt top well.

9. Layer, quilt, and bind as desired.

It's a Great Life

IT'S A GREAT LIFE
by Jan Krentz, 42½" x 42½". Photo by Jan Krentz.
   This barn-raising version of Log Cabin accommodates
photos of all sizes in 8" finished blocks. Jan used Canon
Photo Transfer paper on a Canon 350 at her local Mail Boxes,
Etc., and included both color and black-and-white images.

Yardage Requirements

Block Centers: 1 yard white, finely-woven, 100% cotton fabric for photo transfer

Light Logs: ¾ yard total of light-colored scraps, cut into strips 1" by the width of the fabric.

Dark Logs: ¾ yard total of dark-colored scraps, cut into strips 1" by the width of the fabric.

Inner Border: ¼ yard

Outer Border: ¾ yard

Backing: 1¼ yards

Binding: ½ yard

Batting: 48" x 48"

ASSEMBLING 8" LOG CABIN BLOCKS

First enlarge or reduce your photographs so their dimensions are in whole inches (e.g. 3" x 4", 5" x 5"). Transfer sixteen images to fabric by the photo transfer method of your choice. Be sure to leave at least ½" of space around the transferred images to allow for ¼" seam allowances. Cut out the transferred images including ¼" seam allowance on each side.

You will make a total of sixteen blocks. In an ordinary barn-raising setting, every Log Cabin block can be pieced identically, and the blocks rotated to create the overall pattern of light and dark. However, in this quilt because the center of each block is a photograph, it has a defined top, bottom, left, and right. Therefore, you must pay attention to the relation of the strips to the central photo as you piece.

Make four blocks of each type:

- light strips along the top and right edges of the photo, dark strips along the bottom and left
- light strips along the top and left edges of the photo, dark strips along the bottom and right
- light strips along the bottom and right edges of the photo, dark strips along the top and left
- light strips along the bottom and left edges of the photo, dark strips along the top and right

For one 8" Log Cabin block (see above for color placement):
All seams are constructed with a ¼" seam allowance.

1. With right sides together, sew strip B to the right-hand side of square A (photo).

2. Press toward the darker fabric. Trim the edge even with square A using a rotary cutter.

Quilt Construction

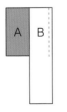

Sew B to A

Press and trim

3. Choose fabric C and place it right sides together with AB unit. Sew across the pieces. Press flat and then press toward the darker fabric. Trim edge using a rotary cutter.

4. Next, sew D to AC side of ABC unit. Press flat and then toward the darker fabric. Trim the edge using a rotary cutter.

5. Continue sewing, pressing, and trimming in a clockwise direction until the block measures 8½" on each side. Add additional logs on any side if necessary.

QUILT ASSEMBLY

7. When you have completed the blocks, arrange them following the quilt photo on page 70.

8. Sew the blocks into rows. Alternate the pressing direction from one row to the next so the seams will lay flat when you sew the rows together.

9. Sew the rows together.

10. Press the top completely. Stay stitch the entire outside edge ⅛" from the edge to keep the blocks from stretching.

INNER BORDER

11. Measure the width of the quilt from side to side across the middle. Cut two borders 1½" wide by the width of the quilt. Pin and sew the borders onto the top and bottom.

12. Measure the length of the quilt from top to bottom across the middle, including the borders you have just added. Cut two borders 1½" wide by the length of the quilt. Pin and sew the borders onto each side.

OUTER BORDER

13. Follow steps 11 and 12 to measure and cut the outer border using 4½" width strips.

14. Press the quilt top well.

Layer, quilt, and bind as desired.

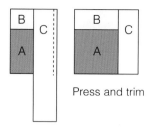

Press and trim

Add C to
AB unit

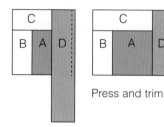

Press and trim

Add D to
ABC unit

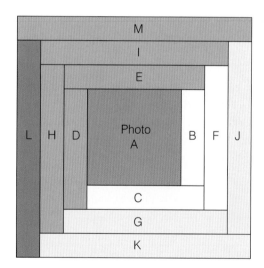

Log Cabin block

Craig Family Album

CRAIG FAMILY ALBUM
by Sharyn Craig, 52½" x 52½".

   Sharyn resized a collection of family photos, both color and black-and-white, by scanning the images into her computer. She enlarged the larger ones to eight inches and reduced the smaller ones to three inches, all square. She used Photoshop and Ofoto scanner software, then fed Canon fabric sheets into her Canon Bubble Jet printer. Twelve-inch Variable Star blocks make up the overall quilt design, with the six-inch blocks set into the sashing. Sharyn made the quilt for her mother-in-law as a tribute and celebration of her life.

Yardage Requirements

Star Centers: 1 yard white, finely-woven, 100% cotton fabric for photo transfer

Large Star Points: scraps to total ¾ yard

Large Star Background: 1⅛ yards

Small Star Points: scraps to total ⅜ yard

Sashing Strips: 1 yard

Outer Border: scraps to total ¾ yard

Backing: 3½ yards

Binding: ½ yard

Batting: 62" x 62"

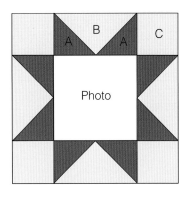

First, enlarge or reduce your photographs as needed. By the photo transfer method of your choice, transfer nine 6" x 6" square images and sixteen 3" x 3" square images. Be sure to leave at least ½" of space around the transferred images to allow for ¼" seam allowances. Cut out the transferred images, including a ¼" seam allowance on each side. You should now have nine 6½" x 6½" squares and sixteen 3½" x 3½" squares, with the image centered on each.

CUTTING 12" SAWTOOTH STAR BLOCKS

For one 12" Sawtooth Star block (make a total of nine):

All seams are constructed with a ¼" seam allowance.

Large Star Points: Cut four 3⅞" x 3⅞" squares, then cut in half diagonally.

Large Star Background: Cut one 7¼" x 7¼" square, then cut in half diagonally, twice. Cut four 3½" x 3½" squares.

PIECING 12" SAWTOOTH STAR BLOCKS

Follow the diagram for piecing the block, pressing the direction of the arrows. Use one of your 8½" image squares as the central square of the block.

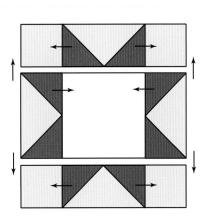

Repeat for a total of nine Sawtooth Star blocks.

CUTTING 3" SAWTOOTH STAR SASHING

Small Star Points: Cut 96 squares 2" x 2".

Sashing Strips: Cut 8 strips 3½" x 42". Cut into 24 strips 3½" x 12½".

PIECING 3" SAWTOOTH STAR SASHING

Following the illustration, sew a 2" square to each corner of each sashing strip. Trim after sewing each square onto the sashing strip, and press toward the star points.

ASSEMBLING THE QUILT TOP

Lay out all of the blocks and sashing following the quilt construction illustration below. Sew the blocks into rows. Sew the rows together.

INNER BORDER

The first border will finish the small stars around the outside edge of the quilt top.

Small Star Points: Cut 16 squares 2⅜" x 2⅜", then cut in half diagonally.
Small Star Background: Cut 16 squares 4¼" x 4¼", then cut in half diagonally twice.

Sew a star point (A) to each short side of a background triangle (B), and press toward the star points.

Border Strips: Cut 12 strips 2" x 12½".

Following the quilt construction illustration, sew a star point/background section to a border strip. Add another star point/background section to the other end of the border strip. Repeat until you have joined four star point/background sections and three border strips. This is the first border for one side of the quilt top. Repeat for the other three sides of the quilt top.

Attach one of the borders to the top edge of the quilt top. Repeat for the bottom border.

Cut 4 squares 2" x 2" for the first border corners. Sew one square to each end of the remaining two borders. Attach these two borders to the sides of the quilt.

OUTER BORDER

Cut 36 rectangles 3½" x 6½". Sew nine of these rectangles end to end. Repeat for the other three borders.

Following the quilt construction illustration, attach the second border to the quilt top. Press the quilt top well.

Layer, quilt, and bind as desired.

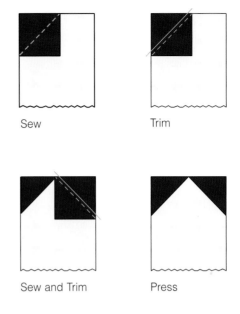

Sew   Trim

Sew and Trim   Press

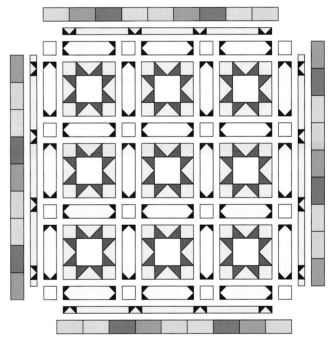

Quilt Construction

Resource List

Transfer Papers

1. Copy shop
2. Arts and Crafts store
3. Fabric or quilt shop
4. Office supply store
5. Computer supply store

6. Air Waves
   Graphics Way
   Lewis Center, Ohio 43035
   614-818-2366

7. Canon
   800-671-1090
   (Canon transfer papers)

8. Data Image
   Monterey Highway, Suite A
   San Martin, CA 95046
   408-686-9065
   408-686-9066
   (Affinity Hot Peel, Affinity
   Cold Peel)

9. Decart, Inc.
   P.O. Box 309
   Morrisville, VT 05661
   800-232-3352
   (call for your nearest supplier of
   Deka Products)

10. Dharma Trading Co.
    P.O. Box 150916
    San Rafael, CA 94915
    800-542-5227
    internet:
    http:/www.dharmatrading.com
    (Magic transfer papers, Retayne,
    Synthropol, and soda ash)

11. Epson
    800-873-7766
    (Epson transfer papers)

12. G & S Dye and Accessories Ltd.
    300 Steelcase Road W., #19
    Markham, ON Canada L3R 2W2
    800-596-0550
    e-mail: gsdye/paro
    (Paro products and transfer papers)

13. Hanes T-Shirts
    6600 Silacci Way
    Gilroy, CA 95020
    888-828-4534
    internet: http://www.hanes2u.com
    (T-Shirt and T-Shirt papers)

14. ProChemical and Dye, Inc.
    P.O. Box 14
    Somerset, MA 02726
    508-676-3838
    800-228-9393
    (Pro-Retayne, other fabric treatments)

15. Stahls' Inc.
    20600 Stephens Street
    St. Claire Shores, MI 48080
    800-622-2264
    800-346-2216 fax
    (transfer papers)

16. TMT North America Inc.
    300 Tri-State International #190
    Lincolnshire, IL 60069
    847-945-9600
    800-624-4210
    (Jet-Wear! transfer paper)

17. Xerox
    800-822-2200
    (Transfer papers for CLC)

Mail Order Photo Transfer Services

Imagination Station
7571 Crater Lake Highway, Suite #101
White City, OR 97503
541-826-7954
800-338-3857

Fabric Fotos
3801 Olsen #3
Amarillo, TX 79108
806-359-8241

Photo Textiles
115 N. College Avenue, Suite 015
Bloomington, IN 47402-3063
800-388-3961
e-mail: phototex@aol.com
internet: http://www.bloomington,in.us/

Photo Sources and Film Service

Library of Congress
Prints and Photos
101 Independence Ave. SE
Washington, D.C. 20540-4730
202-707-5836

Seattle Film Works
Elliott Bay at Pier 89
PO Box 34725
Seattle, WA 98124-9877
800-445-3348
(your film to disk)

On the Internet
Using a search engine such as Yahoo, search for "Public Domain Graphics," Digital Photos," and "Digital Graphics."

The Photographic Arts Center
Stock Photo Desk Book, 4th Ed.
Persky, Robert, exec. ed.
New York, NY
212-838-8640

Bibliography

Some of these books will be available at your local quilt shops.

Simms, Ami. *Creating Scrapbook Quilts*. Mallery Press: Flint, MI 1993.

Ritter, Vivian. *Family Keepsake Quilts: Capturing Memories in Cloth*. Leman Publications/Quilts and Other Comforts: Golden, CO 1991.

Pasquini Masopust, Katie. *Fractured Landscape Quilts*. C&T Publishing, Inc.: Lafayette, CA 1996.

Laury, Jean Ray. *Imagery on Fabric*. C&T Publishing, Inc.: Lafayette, CA 1997.

Heim, Judy and Hansen, Gloria. *The Quilter's Computer Companion*. No Starch Press: San Francisco, CA 1997.

Mail Order

If you are reluctant to leave the chaos and security of your own studio, you can send your photos or drawings off to a mail order company that will produce the transfers for you.

One company, Photo Textiles, uses a chemical process which leaves the fabric quite flexible. Several quilters have particularly mentioned the careful work done by Aneta Sperber, who handles their transfers. Mail order services are provided by Fabric Fotos, Imagination Station, and Photo Textiles.

To receive information from any of the companies, call, write, or e-mail them for details.

Copyright

Copyright Office
Library of Congress
Washington, D.C. 20559
202-707-3000.

index

about the author

As a skilled, insightful, and humorous lecturer and workshop teacher, Jean finds the demands for her time are great. In this book she shares her expertise and viewpoints. Her previous book *Imagery on Fabric* is a favorite among quilters and surface designers.

Jean's recent Silver Star Award at the Quilt Festival in Houston attests to her popularity and to the attention she devotes to each class and to each student. As an exhibiting artist, always short of studio time, Jean insists that soon she will quit "running around" to stay home and concentrate on her own work. In the meantime she'll teach all over, including New York, Florida, and Hawaii, as well as in her hometown.

Jean lives with her husband Frank, a retired professor of art, in the Sierra foothills where they are visited by foxes, wild turkeys, grandchildren, quilters, family, and friends. She continues to write, do commission work, garden a little, read a lot, and keep the silk screen (and bridge cards) moving.

c&t titles

An Amish Adventure, 2nd Edition, Roberta Horton

Anatomy of a Doll, The Fabric Sculptor's Handbook, Susanna Oroyan

Appliqué 12 Easy Ways! Elly Sienkiewicz

Art & Inspirations, Ruth B. McDowell, Ruth B. McDowell

The Art of Silk Ribbon Embroidery, Judith Baker Montano

The Artful Ribbon, Candace Kling

At Home with Patrick Lose, Colorful Quilted Projects, Patrick Lose

Baltimore Album Legacy, Catalog of C&T Publishing's 1998 Baltimore Album Quilt Show and Contest, Elly Sienkiewicz

Baltimore Beauties and Beyond (Volume I), Elly Sienkiewicz

Basic Seminole Patchwork, Cheryl Greider Bradkin

Beyond the Horizon, Small Landscape Appliqué, Valerie Hearder

Buttonhole Stitch Appliqué, Jean Wells

A Colorful Book, Yvonne Porcella

Colors Changing Hue, Yvonne Porcella

Crazy Quilt Handbook, Judith Montano

Crazy Quilt Odyssey, Judith Montano

Crazy with Cotton, Diana Leone

Curves in Motion, Quilt Designs & Techniques, Judy B. Dales

Deidre Scherer, Work in Fabric & Thread, Deidre Scherer

Designing the Doll, From Concept to Construction, Susanna Oroyan

Dimensional Appliqué, Baskets, Blooms & Baltimore Borders, Elly Sienkiewicz

Easy Pieces, Creative Color Play with Two Simple Quilt Blocks, Margaret Miller

Elegant Stitches, An Illustrated Stitch Guide & Source Book of Inspiration, Judith Baker Montano

Enduring Grace, Quilts from the Shelburne Museum Collection, Celia Y. Oliver

Everything Flowers, Quilts from the Garden, Jean and Valori Wells

The Fabric Makes the Quilt, Roberta Horton

Faces & Places, Images in Appliqué, Charlotte Warr Andersen

Fantastic Figures, Ideas & Techniques Using the New Clays, Susanna Oroyan

Focus on Features, Life-like Portrayals in Appliqué, Charlotte Warr Andersen

Forever Yours, Wedding Quilts, Clothing & Keepsakes, Amy Barickman

Fractured Landscape Quilts, Katie Pasquini Masopust

Free Stuff for Quilters on the Internet, Judy Heim and Gloria Hansen

From Fiber to Fabric, The Essential Guide to Quiltmaking Textiles, Harriet Hargrave

Hand Quilting with Alex Anderson, Six Projects for Hand Quilters, Alex Anderson

Heirloom Machine Quilting, Third Edition, Harriet Hargrave

Imagery on Fabric, Second Edition, Jean Ray Laury

Impressionist Palette, Gai Perry

Impressionist Quilts, Gai Perry

Jacobean Rhapsodies, Composing with 28 Appliqué Designs, Patricia Campbell and Mimi Ayers

Judith B. Montano, Art & Inspirations, Judith B. Montano

Kaleidoscopes, Wonders of Wonder, Cozy Baker

Kaleidoscopes & Quilts, Paula Nadelstern

Make Any Block Any Size, Easy Drawing Method • Unlimited Pattern Possibilities • Sensational Quilt Designs, Joen Wolfrom

Mariner's Compass Quilts, New Directions, Judy Mathieson

Mastering Machine Appliqué, Harriet Hargrave

Michael James, Art & Inspirations, Michael James

The New Sampler Quilt, Diana Leone

On the Surface, Thread Embellishment & Fabric Manipulation, Wendy Hill

Papercuts and Plenty, Vol. III of Baltimore Beauties and Beyond, Elly Sienkiewicz

Patchwork Persuasion, Fascinating Quilts from Traditional Designs, Joen Wolfrom

Patchwork Quilts Made Easy, Jean Wells (co-published with Rodale Press, Inc.)

Pieced Clothing Variations, Yvonne Porcella

Pieces of an American Quilt, Patty McCormick

Piecing, Expanding the Basics, Ruth B. McDowell

Plaids & Stripes, The Use of Directional Fabrics in Quilts, Roberta Horton

Quilts for Fabric Lovers, Alex Anderson

Quilts from the Civil War, Nine Projects, Historical Notes, Diary Entries, Barbara Brackman

Quilts, Quilts, and More Quilts! Diana McClun and Laura Nownes

Recollections, Judith Baker Montano

RIVA, If Ya Wanna Look Good, Honey, Your Feet Gotta Hurt..., Ruth Reynolds

Rotary Cutting with Alex Anderson, Tips • Techniques • Projects, Alex Anderson

Say It with Quilts, Diana McClun and Laura Nownes

Scrap Quilts, The Art of Making Do, Roberta Horton

Simply Stars, Quilts that Sparkle, Alex Anderson

Six Color World, Color, Cloth, Quilts & Wearables, Yvonne Porcella

Small Scale Quiltmaking, Precision, Proportion, and Detail, Sally Collins

Soft-Edge Piecing, Jinny Beyer

Start Quilting with Alex Anderson, Six Projects for First-Time Quilters, Alex Anderson

Stripes in Quilts, Mary Mashuta

Through the Garden Gate, Quilters and Their Gardens, Jean and Valori Wells

Tradition with a Twist, Variations on Your Favorite Quilts, Blanche Young and Dalene Young Stone

Trapunto by Machine, Hari Walner

The Visual Dance, Creating Spectacular Quilts, Joen Wolfrom

Wildflowers, Designs for Appliqué & Quilting, Carol Armstrong

Willowood, Further Adventures in Buttonhole Stitch Appliqué, Jean Wells

Yvonne Porcella, Art & Inspirations, Yvonne Porcella

For more information write for a free catalog from:
C&T Publishing, Inc.
P.O. Box 1456
Lafayette, CA 94549
(800) 284-1114
http://www.ctpub.com
email: ctinfo@ctpub.com

Cotton Patch Mail Order
3405 Hall Lane, Dept. CTB
Lafayette, CA 94549
email: cottonpa@aol.com
800-835-4418
925-283-7883
A Complete Quilting Supply Store

notes

the photo transfer handbook